BITE *the* BULLET

Scott Allan is an international bestselling author of 25+ books published in 7 languages in the area of personal growth and self-development. He is the author of *Fail Big, Undefeated,* and *Do the Hard Things First.*

As a former corporate business trainer in Japan, and Transformational Mindset Strategist, Scott has invested over 10,000 hours of research and instructional coaching into the areas of self-mastery and leadership training.

With an unrelenting passion for teaching, building critical life skills, and inspiring people around the world to take charge of their lives, Scott Allan is committed to a path of constant and never-ending self-improvement.

Many of the success strategies and self-empowerment material that is reinventing lives around the world evolves from Scott Allan's 20 years of practice and teaching critical skills to corporate executives, individuals, and business owners.

You can connect with Scott at:
scottallan@scottallanpublishing.com
Visit author.to/ScottAllanBooks to stay up to date on future book releases.

More Inspiring Titles From Scott Allan

Empower Your Thoughts

Empower Your Deep Focus

Rejection Reset

Rejection Free

Relaunch Your Life

Drive Your Destiny

The Discipline of Masters

Do the Hard Things First

Undefeated

No Punches Pulled

Fail Big

Bite the Bullet

Supercharge Your Best Life

Built for Stealth

BITE *the* BULLET

How to Control Your **MIND** and Be **TOUGH**

SCOTT ALLAN

RUPA

Published by
Rupa Publications India Pvt. Ltd 2023
7/16, Ansari Road, Daryaganj
New Delhi 110002

Sales Centres:
Bengaluru Chennai
Hyderabad Jaipur Kathmandu
Kolkata Mumbai Prayagraj

Copyright © Scott Allan 2023

The views and opinions expressed in this book are the author's own and the facts are as reported by him which have been verified to the extent possible, and the publishers are not in any way liable for the same.

All rights reserved.
No part of this publication may be reproduced, transmitted, or stored in a retrieval system, in any form or by any means, electronic, mechanical, photocopying, recording or otherwise, without the prior permission of the publisher.

P-ISBN: 978-93-5702-145-6
E-ISBN: 978-93-5702-146-3

First impression 2023

10 9 8 7 6 5 4 3 2 1

The moral right of the author has been asserted.

Printed in India

This book is sold subject to the condition that it shall not, by way of trade or otherwise, be lent, resold, hired out, or otherwise circulated, without the publisher's prior consent, in any form of binding or cover other than that in which it is published.

CONTENTS

An Introduction   1

Part 1: Why Self-Control Matters   11

Part 2: The Types of Self-Control   39

Part 3: Self-Control and Goal Achievement   59

Part 4: Immediate Gratification and Beating Temptation   73

Part 5: Self-Discipline and Willpower   89

Part 6: Defeating Self-Sabotage   121

Part 7: The 6 Habits of Self-Control   133

Part 8: Managing Energy, Exercise, and Relaxation   151

Conclusion   161

"I can resist everything but temptation."

—Oscar Wilde

AN INTRODUCTION

*"A man without self-control is like a city
broken into and left without walls."*

—Anonymous

Do you struggle with your compulsions? Are you constantly looking for ways to satisfy your 'self' but you're losing the battle? Would you like to be the master of your emotions, instead of a slave to them?

If so, Bite the Bullet will teach you the specific strategies you need to take you from an impulsive addict to a master of self-control.

This book is written to provide you with powerful techniques and strategies to teach you specific strategies for overcoming instant gratification. You will be able to identify the triggers that trap you in the pattern of self-sabotage, and to implement the laws of self-control so you can make better decisions about how to govern your habits that influences behavior.

What does it mean to have self-control?

It is the ability to manage yourself effectively by taking charge of the core areas in your life through conscious decisions followed by the right actions.

What are the right actions?

Those actions where we are doing something that is good for our self-confidence and esteem. The wrong actions would be those choices made in the moment without consideration towards the negative outcome that comes later.

We have all been there. It could be a string of bad habits that you persist in, or an addiction that is in control of your emotions. When we lose the ability to stop a particular activity, especially when it is bad for us, we are mired deep in a compulsive addictive behavior.

A good friend of mine—who struggled for years with immediate gratification and self-sabotaging actions—used to call this biting the bullet. He said, "When you lose the fight to control your own impulses, and you're holding on by your fingertips waiting for the obsession to pass, you are biting the bullet every time." You wind up living a life of precarious existence without any real plan.

The purpose of this book is to share with you the key principles that drive self-control. But I want to make one thing clear. It is not that you are weak or lack willpower. Although willpower has a lot to do with it, willpower alone will not be enough to help you succeed. Willpower is a very powerful influencer in our daily lives. But, you need to back it up with the right strategies to squeeze the most out of it.

Self-control begins with having a clear focus for what it is you want to achieve, and who you want to become in the process. You must be totally honest with yourself and be ready to focus on the areas of your life that you lack all control. Also, it's imperative to make a clear distinction between the things you want to control, but actually can't. These can be outside influences that have nothing to do with you. Or a situational problem that you didn't create but have been pulled into.

The goal is to gain greater self-control over your mind and your environment, and then, scaling up to higher levels of mastery by focusing on what you can directly influence with intentional action.

One of the greatest challenges with this is not trying to control situations or people that extends beyond our circle of influence. As soon as you try to seize control of something that you can't change, this opens up the door for frustration, confusion, self-doubt and chaos. We can only change what we can influence and nothing more.

Now, here are a list of the most common traits that people who struggle with self-control encounter:

- Decision-making
- Overeating
- Addictions
- Lack of Self-discipline
- Low Self-esteem
- Getting stuck
- Confusion
- Lack of clarity on the future
- Feelings of anxiety

What it comes down to is choices. You can have whatever you want if you are willing to make the better choices for it. And, to take it a step further, you recognize the rewards—and consequences—of your immediate impulses versus well-trained choices.

Now, I know what it is like to be stuck in your life, and to feel like you are going no place. And, if you suffer from compulsive impulsiveness, the struggle to get to where you want to be is like trying to drive forward with your car stuck in reverse.

But life doesn't have to be an uphill battle. At least, not every day. There will be days when it is brutal and a real slog just to get through. Days like this can be out of your control, but what this book teaches you is, control what you can with influence, and let the rest go.

If you are caught in a web of anxiety and live in constant fear of the compulsions that drive your mind, the framework in this book is structured to teach you specific strategies for defeating your mind's habit of giving into temptation and instant gratification.

Before we begin, there are a few things we need cover...

Rules of the Game

1. **The ability to self-control your will is an internal job.** It is easy to blame our surrounding environment, people and circumstances on our inability to control ourselves. In a world full of too much stuff, offers everywhere, and the easy access to anything we want a lack of self-control has never been easier. But you don't have to buy into any of it. In this book, I'll show you how to be the master of your emotions, decisions and control your impulses so that you aren't reacting to everything.
2. **You are responsible for your own life…always.** We have been so conditioned to react to our environment, that we have forgotten we really do have complete control over our choices, responses and emotions.

    Doesn't it feel like something is pulling you to react out

of a desire to want something? Well, you don't have to fall victim to this. As I'll show you later on in this book, you're in charge of your life.

You make the choices that govern your earning power, state of health, and overall happiness. This is related to step one where we have to snap out of the world that has convinced us we are powerless.

3. **There is no such thing as a free and easy ride.** Everything has a price. Our compulsive nature has given way to a system of bad habits that are impulsive, out of control, and downright damaging to our lifestyle. But nothing comes for free.

   This out-of-control-behavior that has seized control of our life isn't just a temporary thing. It has taken hold of your emotional state, it controls your decision-making power, and makes you feel like you are a slave to its desires.

   This is the trap that we have fallen into. This is the trap that we will break. Later on, I'll show you how to identify the triggers that are sparking this behavior.

   Bite the Bullet is designed to provide you with empowering tools to overcome your compulsions and gain self-control over your emotional and mental state.

   With this in mind, I believe that you can change, transform, and succeed where you once failed. With this framework, you'll be armed with a specific set of tools to use anytime in even the most desperate of circumstances.

   Instead of feeling "out of control", weak and helpless, you will become in control; in control of your own will, in control of your emotions, and filled with the confidence knowing that you are no longer a slave to someone else's agenda.

Why I Wrote This Book for YOU

Several years ago, I went through a period of anxiety. One of the reasons the doctor said is that, I was never satisfied. That wasn't the reason I was looking for. I was expecting to get some medication, pop a few pills, and be feeling better in a week or two. I did get some meds but also advice from the doctor.

He said: "You are hopelessly trying to gain more in your life through addictive compulsiveness and thinking it will make you happy. If you don't cure that, and stop chasing instant gratification, you'll be miserable for the rest of your days." Those were his exact words.

Most of my actions were devoid of any control, but based on reactive, impulsive decisions without much thought. In other words, I was creating most of my own problems. You see, in many cases, we blame the world around us for our current state. I know I did, and the longer I was convinced the world owed me something, the angrier and more resentful I became.

I listened to his advice and set out to discover the real reason people defeat themselves with compulsive disorders. I was a person whom was constantly trying to achieve, have more, be more, and I wanted it all as fast as I could get it.

Coming from a background and family history of addictive personalities, I had developed what someone called an addiction to "compulsive living'. In other words, I was hooked into feeding a monster that could never be satisfied, whether it was sugar, medication, or any number of addictive habits.

In order to recover, I needed to develop balance, gratitude, and a strategic way of living that wasn't built on a foundation that could crumble underneath my feet at any moment.

What I really wanted, after months of self-searching, was

freedom. I was not free at the time. I had been suffering from self-doubt, low self-esteem, addictive behavior that was spiraling out of control, and the only way to regulate it was to keep all the internal monsters entertained.

It really is a con that we train ourselves to believe in. By thinking that the more we feed into our compulsions will lead to greater self-fulfillment, we are continuously disappointed when repetitive actions lead to the same results.

Freedom is the greatest gift you can give to yourself. But even though we may live in a free society, many people struggle with self-slavery. They are trapped in a system of bad impulsive behavior and compulsive habits robbing them of the life they really want. If you have the desire to change the way you are being controlled by your addictive monkey mind, this book was written for you.

In this book I will cover to some extent the topic of addiction. But, this is not a book for addicts. If that is the case and you struggle with addiction, I would strongly recommend you seek professional help or a support group for addictions that are life threatening. This book can help you to some extent, but it is beyond the scope of recovery from drug, alcohol, or other harmful addictions robbing you of health and happiness.

Now, imagine if you had total control over your life right now? What would you do, think, and feel if you had a life that is your own? Are you tired of being a slave to out of control impulses that are ruining your chances for a happy life?

We do have enough. Yes, even if you don't have as much as the neighbors, when you stop hoarding and trying to fill up your life with empty happiness, the real happiness returns. You don't NEED anything to feel good. I know it may not feel that way right now but...I will show you that there is enough in your life. But it begins with forging the correct mindset towards healing and a willingness to learn and grow.

Our compulsive natures have been set on fire by the world around us. Messages advertising that life should be easy, that we deserve to be happy, and that you shouldn't restrain yourself from owning it today.

In the end, there is always a price to pay. Nothing comes for free in this world. **If you play now, you will pay later.** This isn't just an arbitrary statement; it is the truth. When you give in to the NOW, the immediate gratification, you are optioning to pay LATER. If you borrow money now, you'll pay for it later. If you eat junk food now, you'll pay for it later. If you spend ten hours on the streaming channel instead of exercising and walking, you'll pay for it later.

The question is, do you want to enjoy life now, or enjoy it later? If you're like most people, you said NOW. Of course. We don't know how long we have to live. What if I put off having now for later only to never reach that point in my life where I can enjoy it.

So why can't we have the best of both worlds? What is wrong with having everything now? There is nothing wrong with it, but this is the crux of the issue. How much do you need? What do you need? When do you need it by?

When we can choose to take it or leave it, that is self-control. When we crave something that is pulling at our desires to own, eat or consume, we can say NO.

A Framework for Mastering Self-Control

Bite the Bullet will teach you the system I have been using for years to control—and eventually eliminate—compulsive habits. My habits consisted of online one click shopping, phone swiping, and massive sugar consumption, just to name a few. But, the habit of compulsive addiction is only the symptom. Under the surface was an underlying monster that demanded to be fed.

It would communicate its needs to me through anxiety, fear and cravings. To calm the cravings, I had to take action—in other words, I had to do something that resulted in an emotional high that would last anywhere from a few minutes to a few hours or days.

It was like a rollercoaster. One day I'd be fine, but when the itch came, it demanded everything from me. By creating a system, I was able to bring my compulsions under control, end the bad habits destroying my future, and feel great about who I was and who I am becoming.

Compulsive behavior can be harmless, and harmful. If it's damaging your health, hurting your finances, and draining your emotional well-being, it's time to take intentional action and build in a system for recovery.

Through forming a relationship with your emotions and recognizing why you repeatedly fail—by giving in to your compulsions—you will learn to retrain your brain. Your brain is a massive learning center and it will follow your lead. But you have to lead your mind and set your brain up for success instead of failure.

About Bite the Bullet

This book aims to help you get back your power, control, and confidence in life. It intends to help you understand that you can always choose for yourself and why you must make the most meaningful choice always.

In Bite the Bullet, you will discover:

- the types of self-control, thus helping you understand the concepts better and at a deeper level
- the relationship between self-control and goal fulfillment, along with strategies to materialize all your goals
- the harm of immediate gratification and how to use empowering techniques to beat temptations when you're tempted to act out
- what self-discipline and willpower are, and how you can practice both to live a meaningful and totally fulfilling life
- how to minimize and eliminate self-sabotaging behaviors that get in the way of your self-control, and the ability to live a happy life
- the six primary habits of self-control, and how to implement these habits to push forward through hard times.
- Diverse relaxation techniques and exercises to help you attain, practice and maintain self-control whenever you need it in your personal and professional life.

What I am offering you is the chance to change everything. It doesn't have to take you ten or twenty years either. Within a matter of days, by implementing the action plans and framework in this book, you will learn to make key choices for your life.

Are you ready to break free of your impulsive compulsive self-sabotaging habits?

It begins right here.

PART 1

WHY SELF-CONTROL MATTERS

"If you lose self-control, everything will fall."

—John Wooden

Imagine Where You Could Be…

Can you imagine where your life will be in one year from now once you pivot your mindset? Can you imagine the things you will be able to do and experience, or the places you could visit? How about the physical achievements you desire, such as losing weight or gaining muscle through consistent daily workouts? Or, having control over your mental mastery by governing your thoughts?

Taken for granted, our thoughts are often let alone to run wild, carefree and devoid of any restraint. This allows negative thinking to corrupt our way of living. We become overly stressed, anxious, depressed and fail to gain control of our other areas of life. Paying attention to the details of your thoughts will change the course of your life.

But many people Bite the Bullet on this and they try to control the external circumstances. They lose power when they focus on controlling people or attempting to control the situation. They direct their focus towards people and events outside of their circle of influence.

You can only change what you can control, and you can control your thoughts, actions and choices. You can't control the outcome of your decisions either, but you can make the best choice in the moment based on the information you have.

Anything outside your circle of influence always has elements that are not stable and subject to rapid change. It is like chasing a rabbit when you have a hundred more that are loose.

We all want so many things in this life. To attain what we want, we set various goals and objectives. Unfortunately, even after setting goals, many of us fall short of achieving them. When that happens, we end up blaming different factors involved in the process.

Maybe the timing wasn't right.

Maybe you did not have supportive people around you.

Maybe there was a hint of nepotism that cost you a good job.

Most of us are guilty of playing this blame game at some point or the other in our lives. Unfortunately, as we do so, we somehow forget that our inner power always lies within our control.

We cannot control the external environment, but we can always control our internal environment.

Perhaps your business did not succeed because you did not invest sufficient effort and time into it. Instead of directing time and energy into it, you were busy spending time out with friends. Or watching Netflix. Or combing through the latest Instagram Reels.

Maybe your relationship with your ex-partner did not blossom into something more meaningful and passionate because you could not manage your anger issues.

Perhaps you could not lose weight and follow your passion of becoming a fitness instructor because you kept opting for instant gratification over delayed gratification or because you found easy solace in relaxing more instead of working out daily.

All these factors can have a negative impact towards the pursuit of your life's biggest goals. In fact, most people who fail, usually end up failing on the inside, and this spills over into their external world.

Yes, at times, some unfortunate factors and inevitable forces affect the pursuit of your grandest ambitions. They may even deter us from actualizing our dreams. But when we are steadfast and have absolute clarity on what we want, we materialize our desires no matter what. We will do whatever it takes to get there.

IF we can manage the internal mechanisms of self-control.

I believe the path to building a life that is true to yourself begins with self-regulation.

In its truest sense, self-control comes from understanding what you want, what is right for you, and exercising your control to fulfill those desires. Self-regulation is your capacity to make the right call for yourself in light of your desires and do things that bring you pure joy.

Every time we falter and fail to achieve what we want, we create a brilliant excuse to cover up our lack of willpower. Yes, problems exist all around us, but they are also present for all those who keep embarking on one exciting adventure in life after another, and all those you idealize.

Nobody has an easy or proven path to moving seamlessly through this life. It's hard and it requires the utmost focus and discipline to carve a mindset of stone. What sets accomplished people apart from those who only dream of fulfilling their goals is their ability to exercise self-control, willpower, and implement discipline when it's required.

How does self-control work?

- Self-control empowers you to stay resolute when your temptations dance all around you.
- Self-control empowers you with the strength to get back

up when you fall flat on your face.
- Self-control pushes you the extra mile when your mind and body want to stop and take a break.
- Self-control enables you to break free from the cravings and addictions of unlimited needs the mind and body craves.
- Self-control is your defensive position to overcoming self-defeat.

Your level of self-control helps you stay steadfast when you have to move through a dark tunnel searching for the light.

Challenges ambush everyone; that's a fact of life. All of us go through failures in life, but only those who have empowered their self-control successfully keep their calm in difficult times and power through the difficulties and struggles to create a better life.

White-knuckling it and hoping for the best is not the way to beating temptation. Sooner or later, you give in and then your world caves in.

You wish to be strong, confident, and completely in charge of yourself, thus ensuring that you do what brings you value and meaning and never settle for anything less than what you deserve.

We always have the next plateau top reach, the next level to ascend to. But you must start from where you are, let go of where you have been, and focus on the destination you intend to reach.

One day at a time, one hour at a time. Practicing the discipline of self-regulation means taking care of yourself first and, taking care of the most important garden there is, your own mind.

The Upsell of Self Control

Everyone has an urge to act out on impulsive behaviors. It could be the compulsion to spend cash you don't have, eat food that makes you sick. You could be gambling away the money you just borrowed from the bank, or checking the number of likes on Facebook every five minutes. Whatever it is, an uncontrollable desire to fill yourself up with a stimulating activity has long term—and short term—damaging effects.

To begin our training, let's dive into the reasons **why you need to** work on a process of recovery from your impulsive behavior.

1. Energy: Increased mental and physical energy.

Active compulsions are exhausting. When you are struggling with an (addictive) compulsion, it drains you both mentally and physically. You feel exhausted, as if there is a war going on inside of you. Well, there actually is. The better part of you is resisting the urge to carry out whatever action your compulsive side is trying to tap into.

When you feed into a compulsion, it drains your energy. If you are doing this constantly, halfway through your day, you are already wiped out and just coast through to the end. By gaining control over the compulsion to act out and do something, by feeding into your compulsive self, you are wasting creative energy and draining your energy that could be put towards something else.

2. Abundance: Make Positive Gains with an Abundant Lifestyle.

Abundance comes in many forms. There is the abundance of love, having things, more money, and the abundance of time. As we gain greater control of our lives, this invariably boosts our opportunity to live more abundantly.

We can have more abundance in money that isn't spent on sudden compulsions to gamble or shop; we have an abundance of energy for living when we are no longer giving into our weaker habits.

Abundance creates a fuller, richer lifestyle.

3. Freedom: You'll experience a sense of freedom that you've never had

Feeling trapped and like there is no end to your misery? If you are trapped by instant gratification cycle you are going to feel trapped, doomed and helpless. I know, I felt this way for many years. But as you develop better habits and adhere to the laws of greater self-control, you will tap into your freedom in greater ways.

Many people, when they are trapped in the pattern of compulsive disorder, feel like prisoners in their own minds and bodies. It's a terrible feeling. How can we be happy when under the strict influence of such a powerful enemy? But that's what it is: a trap. By breaking free, you are taking a leap towards freedom.

Can you image a life free of compulsions and always feeding into your mind's addictive behavior? Can you visualize the person you could become right now by committing to a higher path that won't fail you?

A life of compulsive behavior will fail you. You will forever be playing a game that you can't make the rules up for. After living a life of compulsivity, I realized that everything I was doing was being controlled by some sudden impulse. It was always a decision driven by an emotion that was attached to a compulsive disorder demanding something.

Until I cut the cord on that, I was living a life of lies, and freedom was a dream. Now I'm living the dream and the lies are gone. In this book I will show you who to do this, because it isn't as difficult or impossible s you might be thinking.

4. Confidence: Gain greater confidence through self-control

A loss of control is going to suck your confidence away. But as you gain greater clarity at what you want, confidence increases. Confidence is the result of feeling good about yourself.

As long as you are stuck, you will never be free, and if you're not living your life but are victim to something else controlling it, your self-esteem, image and confidence will suffer. In this book I will cover confidence building strategies but, know this now that, you are in control of how confident you feel.

You don't have to wait for a big win or to succeed at something before having confidence. You don't have to earn it; it's yours. Give it to yourself right now. Tell yourself that YES, I am good enough for anything.

5. Patience: Patient people are also mood regulators

Have you ever met an impatient person that had to have everything right now? Of course, children can be this way.

When they want something on the spot they cry, and then mom or dad has to decide to give it to them. But you see, this creates a habit and sets up the response system that we still remember later on in life. If I cry, I'll get what I want.

As children, it is cute and forgiving. But for an adult making a living, trying to function in the world, when you don't get what you want, and lacking the patience to wait or prolong the pleasure, you are tapping into that childhood memory when you acted and were rewarded.

Patient people have a firm display of their emotions. They can control the urge to take right away. They can spend two minutes in line without pulling out their phone and checking for messages for the fifth time in less than five minutes.

Patience is, to use an old acronym, a virtue. But more than that, patience is a skill. If you can build up your patience, you'll also become more tolerant and you will be able to regulate your mood.

Impatient people are moody. They can be difficult to be around because it turns out to be all about THEM and their NEEDS not being met right now. I want it, I deserve it, and I need it right now. This lends to selfish self-centeredness and then, we are closing the loop back to repeating the compulsive behavior again.

6. Compulsivity Leads to Negativity

When we feel overwhelmed by our desires and unable to hold ourselves back, there is a rush of shame and guilt afterwards. These feelings can turn into negative thoughts that beat you up for doing the thing that you swore you wouldn't do.

This book is about finding the right balance between your

compulsive behavior [ongoing wants and needs] and your ability to develop stronger self-control skills. It would be unrealistic to expect you to completely eliminate compulsive behavior, not to mention stressful.

We are human, and there is an underlying need for us to want, desire and give in to our cravings. So, what we are talking about here is a balance between what we crave and how to regulate our compulsions to acting out of control. For example, if you are hooked on junk food [chocolate, chips, ice-cream, etc.…] and this is causing health problems [overweight, diabetes, etc.…] it is a problem. But what identifies this as a problem is your desire to stop and you can't.

You really want to go to the gym and start working out again, or join that hot yoga class, or run in a marathon. But, you opt instead for feasting on junk and television, and this kills your ambition. Psychologically, you are beating yourself down and reinforcing the behavior that's blocking you from what you do want.

The same can be said for wealth. You desire more money in your pocket, but you can't stop 1-clicking, or gambling on the next horse race. Rest assured that, no matter what your big goal is, if you are struggling to achieve this goal, it's probably a compulsive behavior that is. Derailing your efforts.

This is where our skills in self-control and discipline will come into play. By building your self-control muscle, you will be able to combat the fatigue and feelings of helplessness you experience when you try to say NO. Instead of taking action towards the wrong things, you can feel confident by taking action towards what truly matters.

When compulsion becomes a problem is when it interferes with the lifestyle that we want to build. There is a difference between surrendering and giving up. When you surrender, you are opening your mind to the greater possibilities without struggling against the resistance. In giving up, we are throwing in the towel and letting our weaker selves fall under the impulses that are ruling and ruining the quality lifestyle that we could be enjoying.

I want you to imagine with a clear sense of visual detail the confidence you will have when you are able to exercise control over your life. What personal reinvention will you discover when you are living more abundantly, with high-octane physical and mental energy fueled by the know-how that you are overtaking the weaker impulses that have been pulling and twisting your destiny into something you never wanted.

By eliminating the non-essentials, we are left with the greater parts of a better whole. Your actions are a direct correlation of your thoughts. If our thinking is in any way negative or distracted by the many non-essentials such as watching TV for hours at a time while your goals remain untouched, you are going to develop deep stress, anxiety and possibly depression.

Years ago, when I was going through a very dark time, I would hide from the reality of the situation by staying tuned out. The problem with this is, when we tune out of the problem, we cannot discover the solution to making anything better. You will only achieve the impossible if you make the hard choices and stay with the course that is guaranteed to bring you success.

You may have many bad habits, as we all have, but it is probably only a select few that are damaging your self-esteem and motivation. For myself, my big impulsive habit was turning on the TV when I was bored, tired, or stressed. I used it as a means to tune out.

In many instances, our compulsive habits are nothing more than broken or worn-down habits. But without a set stagey or plan to break away from these broken habits, we remain trapped in their patterns of defeat. In other words, when you are stuck and you continuously feed the beast, you are biting the bullet every time. It is like force feeding yourself poison when you no it's not good for you, but you do it anyway.

In this training, I will walk you through the steps to eliminate the compulsive actions that are blocking you from achieving your goals, and then, show you how to build self-control through the locus of control method and adopting the laws of self-control. Combining actionable tasks with a stronger sense of focus, we can move ahead, crush the opposition/resistance, and feel greater about ourselves as we get to focus on what matters.

According to experts and successful people, self-control is one of the most important virtue you need to work on. It is the formula and solution to raising optimism and living your dreams by maximizing your potential.

From athletes to inventors, to business moguls to motivational speakers, to artists and trainers and to scientists and writers to every person who has had a good taste of success and made a mark for themselves has been able to do so through the practice of self-control.

The good thing is, you are soon going to be amongst that lot, too, because very soon, you too will have complete control over yourself and truly empower your self-control.

Whether it's that of attaining self-control, any goal has a strong foundation in the benefits it creates. You only work for things that promise you some gains or wins. The same rule applies to building self-control.

Why Self Control Matters

To become truly motivated to develop your self-control, and then exercise it every time there is a need for it, you first need to understand why it truly matters as much as it does.

Self-control matters because:

It helps you keep your emotions in check

A lack of self-control is associated with impulsive behaviors and emotions. Lacking the capacity to control yourself greatly means that you cannot keep your emotions in check. You often behave erratically, which impacts you and those around you in one way or the other.

Think of a toddler who does not hesitate to throw a tantrum the instant his parent does not agree to something he wants. He behaves impulsively, starts wailing, and may even throw things around. While toddlers are in the process of regulating their emotions and rationally responding to situations when they don't get things their way, those with a lack of self-control tend to behave similarly.

Being easy to agitate, resorting to yelling and misbehaving with others, and becoming controlling when people don't abide by your rules are issues that stem from an absence of self-control.

When you cannot regulate your emotions, you let them run wild, and that's when you develop behavioral and temperamental issues. These issues interfere with your personal life, professional endeavors, and relationships.

However, all of this changes for the better when self-control comes into the equation. As you become better aware of what self-control is and what it entails, you understand the importance of keeping your cool when things don't go your way and how to respond to situations in better ways that drive you towards getting the desired results.

Consequently, you become successful in keeping a tighter leash on your emotions, which helps you think clearly and rationally before putting your foot down. Instead of allowing your anger, envy, sadness, joy, and any intense emotion to guide your decisions, you let them calm down and then think logically on the best way to go about a specific decision.

It helps you make informed decisions

One of the most significant benefits of exercising self-control is that it develops your ability to make well-informed, rational, and meaningful decisions.

Most of the time, we cannot do what we want and objectify our goals because we make hasty decisions. Something appears shiny, and we head straight for it, assuming it to be gold, with our wallets open ready to buy, hungry for the next method or course that can change everything. Unfortunately, after holding it, we realize how it was only an illusion.

Hasty decisions always get the better of us, which is why it is crucial to think calmly and rationally.

When you can keep your emotions in check, and temptations at a distance, you can analyze the situation logically, weigh the pros and cons of each option, understand what works best, and then put your best foot forward. This happens when you understand that you have that power within yourself to take action towards the best course of action based on a decision made through a logical process.

It helps you combat your temptations

One of the biggest hurdles in the pursuit of our goals is giving in to our temptations. We all have different temptations. These distractions sidetrack us from our goals and lure us towards things that may seem easy and pleasurable, but only for the short term. Temptations are always transitory; they keep us from doing things that bring us genuine empowerment.

We find it easy to surrender to our temptations because we lack self-control. Eating a big bowl of spaghetti when you should be eating a salad feels right only when you lack self-restraint. The instant you get your power back, you can refuse the bowl of spaghetti and enjoy your salad because you know it is the right choice for you.

It ensures you keep the bigger picture in clear sight

Exercising consistent self-control gets the job done by helping you keep the bigger picture in sight. When you give in to distractions—and get sidelined by a shiny object—you can lose sight of your primary goal.

We forget what regular exercise will lead to, what may happen if we work hard for 10 hours a day, or how our business will flourish if we spend more time on it instead of "chilling with Netflix." All of this changes for the better when self-control comes into play.

Self-control defines the importance of your goals and helps you stay focused on the primary target despite the distractions that ambush you from time to time. With the bigger picture clearly formulated in your mind, and with a profound realization of its importance and value in your life, you find it easier to progress towards—and ultimately achieve—your big goal.

It enforces delayed gratification over instant gratification

Delayed gratification refers to the practice of waiting to get a positive return or a win in the long term. You are postponing the present moment pleasure for future enjoyment. You're not eating the marshmallow now but, are willing to put in the time to savor it for later. In contrast, instant gratification refers to opting for whatever brings you pleasure, joy, comfort, or convenience right now (in the short term).

When you pursue instant gratification, you opt for whatever seems easier to you in the short term. You opt in for enjoying immediate gains delivered right now instead of waiting for potentially better gains later. However, when you prioritize delayed gratification over instant gratification, you accomplish what you truly want and get bigger gains in the long run.

Many of us fall short of accomplishing our aims because we give into delayed gratification. Sleeping in daily seems like an easier and more comfortable choice than going for a run or waking up early to work more, so we choose the former. But when you run daily or work harder regularly, you get that athletic physique you have always wanted.

The promotion you've been holding out for one day becomes yours. Instead of quitting too soon to pursue other immediate opportunities, you make a choice to take a chance, work harder, dig in deeper and make it all happen.

With self-control, you realize the importance of pursuing delayed gratification over instant gratification because you understand how the former is more beneficial for you than the latter, and helps you achieve what you want.

Delayed gratification empowers your life because you can make the right choices you have always wanted to, do things as you desire, and not allow your momentary whims to control you every time.

It encourages you to make healthier choices

A life characterized by self-discipline is a healthy and happy life.

Most of us make unhealthy choices when we haven't shaped our self-restraint to align with what truly matters, our biggest dreams and aspirations.

We sleep too late or barely sleep at all because we don't know when to draw the line between working hard and exhausting ourselves We tend to sleep more when we don't understand how oversleeping every day can make us sluggish, thus paving the way for a sedentary life.

We find comfort in eating junk food, processed meats, sugar, and calorie-rich foods when we fail to think about their harmful effects. We eat in a rush when we don't acknowledge how slow eating promotes satiation and enjoyment.

We don't exercise or move around much because we cannot see how staying inactive impacts the quality of our life.

We keep making unhealthy choices because we cannot say no to ourselves when the need to do so arises.

From not exercising to not sleeping well to not eating healthy, we make many poor and choices when we don't practice self-control. This leads to a weakening of willpower and motivation as the pursuit for higher levels of dopamine rises.

As you will discover in this book, your life becomes

healthier, richer, calmer, and more meaningful when practicing self-control delivers everything you have ever wanted...and so much more.

That's when you start to assess your decisions and their ramifications in your life to make better choices every time. Naturally, that improves the quality of your life, and you start to move closer towards the desired vision that encompasses all the great things you have the potential of becoming.

It helps you discover your purpose in life

Many of us have come to a point in life when we felt our lives lacked meaning. This lack of connection and meaning comes from not identifying your purpose in life.

Your purpose in life does not have to be something extraordinary or miraculous. It can be providing value to others through your organic food venture or being a good teacher to your students. However, when you discover it, you realize your true potential and purpose.

With an understanding of your mission, you develop a clear direction to pursue your life's true calling. When that is the case, you know what brings you fulfillment, making it easier to make the right choices that align with your journey.

Making this discovery is possible when you practice self-restraint. Do you know why? When you cannot control random thinking, follow your whims, set meaningless goals based on transitory desires, and give in to your impulsive urges, you struggle to focus on what truly matters for you.

When you combat your temptations, control meaningless desires, manage your emotions, and think clearly, you align your thoughts, and emotions with intentional action that is goal-focused. This is a better approach to reacting out of scarcity or impulse.

It makes you empathetic

Recently conducted researches show that *empathy and self-control* are regulated by the same region of the human brain: the right temporoparietal junction, aka rTPJ.

The study conducted—by Alexander Soutscheck—shows that, when you shut down the rTPJ part of the brain, it inhibits your ability to practice self-control and empathy.

You may have noticed how compassionate you become towards others when you start to exercise better self-restraint in resistance to distraction and other temptations. That's possible because you understand your struggle to combat your temptations and realize how others may experience the same. This realization makes you empathize with others and nurture a kind heart to help those in need.

It helps you develop deeper focus

Deep focus is paramount to success. Whether your target is to become the employee of the week, read 10 books a month, lose 40 pounds this year, or 10x your business sales this quarter, you need to focus on your big goal to turn your vision into a reality.

Without focus, almost everything is impossible, and laser focus comes only from developing your capacity to stay steadfast when temptations lure you away. You know what you aspire for better than anyone, and you stay focused and in flow to achieve it. That's when you do everything required to achieve that goal and let go of everything else that takes you away from it.

Build Hard Grit

Grit is one of the most important ingredients to succeed in life. No matter what your aspirations are and the ideas you have for your ideal life, you can achieve it if you are gritty enough to bear the daily grind and keep powering through towards your goal.

Grit is about being resilient, persevering in hard times, being optimistic about the future, and creatively finding solutions to your problems. When mixed together, all these ingredients build hard grit, and that's what you develop when you exercise your willpower.

With self-discipline, you stay strong when the going gets too tough, do not give into adversities, stay positive in the bleakest of times, and think outside the box to create new possibilities where none existed for you. That's how you build grit, and that's how you achieve what you believe is rightfully yours.

As you will learn in Bite the Bullet, managing your own self-control is not as complicated as you might think it is. Rather, the obstacle is to break down limiting beliefs holding you back from believing you actually can win over your weaker impulses.

Right now, I want you to recognize one fact: Your addiction to impulsive disorder is winning because you give into the temptation. Like the rope that becomes frayed over time, your willpower has become weakened because it's continually losing. Now is the time for you to begin stacking up small wins.

Grit is built brick by brick, with one habit stacked onto another, practicing the strategies that move you away from giving into temptations and building a stronger wall for protection.

Pushing Beyond Failed Strategies

Before I get into the material that outlines the strategies that work, let's take a quick look at the techniques we tried that failed.

You will recognize these because they are the most common and often misunderstood myths that, in order to change an impulsive or bad habit, we have to suffer through it. I don't believe that suffering has to be part of the plan. You can have your cake and eat it too, but just not in the way that you think.

When we try to stop the bad habits from taking away our health, wealth and freedom, we begin by laying down the law. We decide that enough is enough and that we've had enough of this addictive habit, impulsive action or negative thought pattern. Whatever it is that you are tired of repetitively doing and getting the same result, you have now concluded to pivot and change it. But we end up failing when we start this by making promises to ourselves that we can't keep.

We say things like:

- I'll never do that again
- I'm done with this
- Starting tomorrow I am going to…
- I'll have just one more and then…
- I can control this anytime I want…

But the cycle continues.

You have your own valid excuses. But the problem with this is, these convictions that we make, although with the best intentions, are setting us up for disappointment. Change isn't easy, but it isn't as difficult as we make it out to be, either.

We set up ourselves up to fail by:

1. Swearing off the habit altogether. We have all been there. That day of decision where we say to our spouse or friends: "That's it, I'm done with that. Never again!" Only the next day, or the following week, we are back to the same pattern, only this time it is worse.

Now you are beating yourself up for being such a failure. You have proven that you are weak and that you can't change because of lack of willpower. Why? Well, it is simple science actually. If you decide to replace a behavior, you need a new, improved set of actions to replace it. Otherwise, you end up obsessing over the compulsive action that you just swore you'd quit.

Later on, we will also look at how motivation plays a big part in this. When our motivation is strong we can do anything. But after a day at work, your willpower is depleted, and you can't resist giving in to your weaker compulsions. This isn't a sign of being weak but a sign of being human. Later we will look at how to manage willpower.

2. Focusing on short-term satisfaction. It comes down to a reward system. We are seeking some form of pleasure through our habits and behavior patterns. If we go without this reward, that feeling that we are denying ourselves something creeps in. It sticks like glue.

You go to war with your mind as you wrestle with the idea of should I or shouldn't I? You feel guilty for not feeding your desires. This is when your willpower gets cut down and eventually fails you.

3. Making false promises that "I'll control it someday. Just not today." We lie to ourselves when we try to take up a new habit, only to fall back on the old habit several days or weeks later. We cope with our failure by making a false promise that someday we will change. Someday will be different. Someday I'll have enough courage, confidence or motivation to change the way I have been behaving.

But what if that someday never comes. What if today is the only day and there is nothing else. What if you had 24 hours to change everything, what would you do?

Would you waste the last hours of your life trapped in your repetitive cycle of shame and defeat? The promise that we will put an end to it is a false promise that rarely come true. We just want to believe it. It acts as an excuse for never doing anything. If you want to make a promise to yourself, promise to not put off doing anymore, and swear to take intentional action on the spot when it is called for.

4. We don't reward ourselves when we succeed. We know what it is like when we cave in and give into that compulsion. The reward is what we get when we indulge. But what about the reward when we exercise control for the first day, or the next day? What do you do for yourself when you succeed in stopping a compulsive behavior? Later in the book we will look at the reward system you need to make the effort worth it. You will learn to reward yourself everyday with something instead of it always being a rush or fulfilling some instant craving to gratification.

In order to get beyond the compulsive behaviors and bad habits that have taken hold of your life, you should think about the reward system that you've set up for yourself. To change, we need a new set of rewards, and they have to be as equally powerful as the reward, stimulus or sense of euphoria you feel when you take part in an impulsive or addictive action.

Here is an example. For years I was addicted to internet shopping. I couldn't go online without buying something on Amazon or eBay. Within a few years I had gone through most of my savings, and had filled up my house with toys, collectables, and loads of stuff that I later didn't need. I was living in a life of clutter driven by the compulsion to spend more and have more.

I had lost sight of my goals and had traded them in for less. My reward was the feeling of euphoria when that package arrived in the mail, or even the sense of excitement as a I hit the BUY NOW button.

When I realized that it had become a problem, because the credit card bills were being paid late or not at all, I recognized that something had to change. I was hooked into the short-term reward of filling up my life with things I thought I needed. Meanwhile, goals went unfulfilled and, in the end, I ended up broke. But I had lots of stuff.

Fast forward several years later and when I switched gears, I sold everything, got serious about my goal of becoming a bestselling author, and abandoned that path that would have ruined everything.

How about you, are you stuck in a similar situation? A habit that is holding you back? You've tried to quit many times but couldn't?

As you progress through this book, I assure you that you will find yourself making better and healthier decisions in life. I also promise you that this book will prove revolutionary in your life because it intends to help you empower your self-control for the better.

While this may seem like a big claim, as you continue reading and implementing the lessons you will learn from this self-control guide, you will experience a real, personal impact that will motivate you to keep reading and implementing what you learn.

In the next chapter, you will get a better understanding of the different types of self-control. More importantly, I will teach you how to manage your emotions and make the best choices without confusion or uncertainty.

"To establish true self-esteem, we must concentrate on our successes and forget about the failures and the negatives in our lives."

—Denis Waitley

PART 2

THE TYPES OF SELF-CONTROL

*'He who controls others may be powerful,
but he who has mastered himself is mightier still.'*

—Tao Te Ching

There is a certain sense of power attached to controlling others and dominating them. That said, "true might" comes from mastering yourself.

Indeed, controlling others makes you dominant over them, but it does not really help you win their love, respect, and admiration, especially if you negatively control them. Contrarily, when you control yourself, you become a responsible, confident, and gritty individual with a very enigmatic personality. Your personality then works like a magnet that attracts other people towards you, especially the people you need to push forward on this journey.

I am quite sure you want to have a charismatic personality and achieve all your goals in life. To help you move closer to this goal, let cultivate a better understanding of the different kinds of self-control.

Impulse Control

As the name suggests, this type of self-control relates to your impulses and impulsive behaviors. It is about controlling your impulses and having the ability to stop and think things through before taking a step forward. Impulse control teaches you to respond and not react to situations.

What happens when you lack impulse control

We often react to situations, let our emotions control us illogically, and succumb to our whims and temptations.

Consider the following examples:

- Buying a bar of chocolate at the cash register when getting your groceries billed
- Yelling at your kid because she dropped a bowl of soup on the floor;
- Buying tons of clothes at a sale even though you don't need it and leaving your job just because your boss admonished you?

What do these examples have in common? They are all examples of reacting to your impulses.

When you lack impulse control, you tend to experience the following issues in your life:

- You rush through projects
- You behave irascibly with people when they disagree with you
- You make irrational decisions when things don't go your way
- You interrupt others when they are talking
- You make impulsive purchases, most of which turn out to be useless
- You are inconsistent with your work and habits
- You jump to conclusions quickly without analyzing things deeply or objectively

When such problems exist in your life, naturally, it becomes difficult to make up your mind regarding what you want. However, impulse self-control mitigates this.

How impulse self-control improves things

Impulse self-control allows you to put a leash on your impulsive reactions. Every time you experience a certain situation, you take stock of your needs and the environmental factors and then use them to put your best foot forward.

Also, you learn to explore and understand your genuine needs, which ensures that you only opt for things you want. This helps you make healthier and wiser decisions regarding your health, nutrition, fitness, purchases, work, and even relationships.

Moreover, all types of self-control teach you to respond and not react to situations which is a huge benefit.

How self-control helps you respond and not react to situations

> *'Not to have control over the senses is like sailing in a rudderless ship, bound to break to pieces on coming in contact with the very first rock.'*
>
> —Mohandas Gandhi

If you have ever observed yourself in different situations, especially the unprecedented, volatile ones, you would have noticed how you react to each one of them.

What is reacting, you may ask?

Reacting to things refers to giving in to your impulsive urges. For instance, you may have a heated discussion with your friend, and he says something nasty to you. You feel like replying to him with an abusive remark. In case you do that, that is you reacting to the situation.

Usually, when we lack control, especially impulse and emotional self-control, which we shall discuss below, we react to different situations. We end up giving in to our emotional and temperamental urges that make us resort to illogical decisions, most of which don't pan out well for us.

Perhaps you're having a great time with your current girlfriend and decide to move in with her to please her. Only a few days later, you realize that both of you weren't yet ready for this move.

Maybe you jump to the offer of partnering up for a business with your best friend. After struggling to co-operate with each other for a while and function as a pair, you realize you only reacted to your impulses.

Reacting to your impulses, emotions, bodily movements, situations, and experiences in life is not a very wise move. All of us have been down that rabbit hole at some point in our lives. While it is alright to err and falter, it is equally important to learn from your mistakes and use them to improve yourself and your life.

The most appropriate and rational approach to making decisions is to respond and not react to situations.

Responding to situations is quite the opposite of reacting. It involves a careful, deliberate, and objective assessment of the situation and your thoughts, emotions, desires, and needs. Responding is about examining the situation you have encountered, how it has influenced you, and what you genuinely want, thereby figuring out the best way to handle it.

Let's continue using the example of having a fiery debate with your friend. Mid-argument, you may feel like abusing your friend; however, you choose to hold on to that remark. Instead of letting it all out, you cope with your anger and control your emotions and impulses, and even bodily movements if the need be.

You may excuse yourself from the moment, take deep breaths, and calm yourself down, and only when you feel your intense, volatile emotions have cooled off, you think of the best possible manner to reply to your friend.

Similarly, because you choose to respond instead of blatantly reacting to different life episodes, you end up making rational, meaningful, and worthwhile decisions in life.

Emotional Control

Emotional control refers to keeping your emotions under check, thereby ensuring that they do not get the better of you in one way or the other. When you are emotionally controlled, you can manage your feelings better, which keeps you from becoming too upset and losing your calm when unexpected things happen.

To develop a firmer understanding of how emotional self-control can help you, let us discuss how its absence affects your life.

What happens in the absence of emotional control

Lacking emotional self-control means you have very limited control over your emotions. Human beings are quite emotional creatures. We have eight basic emotions: *trust, surprise, joy, sadness, envy, anger, fear,* and *disgust*, and these core emotions further shape scores of other emotions.

When we experience a certain emotion, we often hold on

too tightly to it. The longer an emotion stays inside us, the stronger it becomes, and that's how it makes us react to different situations. You may lash out at your co-worker because of the suppressed anger you have been holding on to for a long time. Perhaps you become withdrawn because of all the sadness you have been bottling up for a while.

Without any emotional control, you turn into an emotional wreck who makes rash decisions and lets emotions get in the way of doing meaningful things in life, including achieving your goal and passion and fulfilling your potential.

- You may find yourself easily losing your temper.
- Frustration is likely to become a constant part of your life.
- Every time the going gets tough, you may give up on something you truly want.
- You may also struggle with handling criticism well. Even when you receive constructive criticism, you may react to it, making matters worse for yourself.
- When things take an unexpected turn, you may become very agitated.
- Lack of emotional control also makes it tougher to calm yourself down when you become furious with yourself or others.
- Your emotions also interfere with your ability to concentrate on tasks and get things done on time.
- You are likely to have many unsettled feelings inside you that keep stirring up intense emotions, making it difficult for you to be happy with yourself and your life.

These are all substantial problems that most certainly interfere with your well-being and quality of life.

Emotional control makes you poised and confident

Fortunately, with emotional control, you can overcome all these issues and shape yourself into the composed, tranquil and self-aware individual you have always wanted to become. As you learn better ways to manage your emotions, you understand how to prevent them from becoming volatile, which helps you stay serene almost always, especially when you need to approach something calmly.

Moreover, you also learn the art of letting go of pent-up emotions, which ensures that you don't keep holding on to them for good and instead release the inner frustration to promote calmness in your body, mind, and spirit.

With better emotional control, you find it easy to focus on tasks, handle and improve your lack of confidence, become a loving person to be around, and regulate your emotions better to ensure they don't override your judgment and thinking skills.

Movement Control

Movement self-control refers to having a better ability to control how your body moves around. It's regulating your physical movements and reactions better, so you make certain not to behave inappropriately with anyone.

It may not seem a very monumental problem to you right now, but movement self-control can have far-reaching implications. When you have movement control, you find it easy to keep yourself calm and composed and behave appropriately most of the time.

What happens when you lack movement control?

In the absence of movement control, you are bound to face several issues.

- You may find yourself being extremely restless.
- You may also have trouble controlling your energy and, at times, become extremely active without knowing how to let out that energy in the most positive and useful manner.
- You may at times react in a volatile manner, throw things around, and even hit people.
- You are likely to have a very tactile demeanor where you express your sentiments by slapping people on the arm or being pushy at times.
- You may also interrupt and disrupt conversations and games while engaging with others.

It is crucial to control such behaviors to ensure that they don't get in the way of your routine functioning and do not keep you from behaving appropriately and respectably with others.

As you learn to build movement self-control, you understand how reactive you may get in bodily movement and train yourself to tame such behaviors. Resultantly, you become calmer and express yourself calmly without being disruptive and volatile with others. This demeanor naturally helps you foster better relationships with loved ones.

Concentration Self-Control

The last type of self-control we shall focus on is concentration control, which, as the name suggests, relates to your ability to concentrate on tasks.

A commonly experienced problem that even attacks the better of us is a lack of focus. We find ourselves losing focus in our routine and substantial tasks, easily giving in to our distractions. Divided concentration makes it incredibly tough to do tasks well, focus well on them, and perform to the best of our abilities.

Concentration control allows you to break free from these challenges. It allows you to control your ability to understand tasks and fully concentrate on them, thereby ensuring that you perform as expected or even better and attain the desired results.

What happens when you lack concentration control?

In the absence of concentration control, you often struggle with the following issues:

- You constantly experience an inability to focus on a given task or a chore you assigned to yourself
- You cannot grasp hold of basic instructions pertinent to a task
- You work on tasks for a little bit and become distracted by other meaningless tasks or more pleasurable activities
- You easily lose interest in your work
- You forget important tasks or what you ought to do in a given situation
- You don't know how to commence and progress with different activities
- You experience difficulty processing information easily
- You take longer than expected to complete chores
- You easily postpone tasks and give them a longer deadline

- You procrastinate on substantial and seemingly difficult tasks
- You set goals but never really accomplish them
- You quit goals midway through
- You feel lost in life and struggle to get clarity on what you truly want
- You become agitated easily with the slightest change in plans or any unexpected disruptions
- You easily lose sight of the bigger picture and instead engage in pointless activities
- You pursue instant gratification over delayed gratification
- You complain a lot about a lack of fulfillment and meaning in life

These are all substantial problems that pave the way for more significant life issues and problems. The good news is that concentration control helps you resolve all these issues and get yourself and your life back on track.

How concentration self-control improves your life

As you attain the other three types of self-control, your concentration control improves too. The reality is that all these types of self-control have a close kinship. You need emotional control, impulse self-control, movement control, and concentration control to perform well in any area of life and commit yourself to your goals to the point that you successfully execute them. One does not simply exist without the other.

As you build concentration control, you will find it easier to focus on your tasks. You will comprehend them better, discern between high priority and low priority tasks, process guidelines better, and actively work on what you need to do to move yourself and your life forward.

Instead of surrendering to your urge to procrastinate, you will figure out ways to make your work manageable, thereby ensuring that you get straight to business, finish your tasks timely, and rev up your productivity.

When working on a task, you are 100% involved in it with complete concentration and are emotionally, mentally, and physically present. That's how you perform well at it and get the desired results.

Later in the book, we shall discuss many strategies to help you develop all these kinds of self-control. For now, here is an activity for each of the four types of self-control explained above.

This simple exercise will help you start training in these areas, thereby getting a better grasp on your movements, emotions, concentration, and impulses.

Exercise for Impulse Self-Control

- If you are currently experiencing a strong urge to do something, focus on that. Write down what that impulsiveness is and what it is urging you to do.
- Think of what that impulsiveness stems from and why it is making you feel a certain way. For instance, if you are on a diet plan, and you just came across an ad for a new fast food eatery in your area that makes you order a huge juicy beef burger with some fizzy drink and a brownie, why do you think you feel that way? Is it because you have been going too hard on yourself following this diet regimen? Or is it because you feel hungry? Whatever your situation is, explain it here.

- Now, think of how reacting to this impulse can harm you or disrupt your future plans. Continuing with the example of dieting, think of how ordering a calorie-rich meal can disrupt your diet and keep you from attaining that slender physique you want and becoming healthier, which is something you truly want to achieve. Write down your feelings here.
- Take a few deep breaths, inhaling from your nose to a count of 4 and exhaling from your mouth to a count of 6. The more you exhale, the calmer you feel. Do this for a full minute. Even set a timer to keep track of time. Once done, write down how you feel about that impulse now. Rate it on a scale of 0 to 10, with 10 being the highest intensity. Describe your findings here.
- Now think of the most logical way to behave in this situation. What do you think is the right measure to take? Should you order a burger or a salad? Or how about distracting yourself by fixing up a meal yourself from the groceries in the kitchen. Write down your ideas here.
- Once you have a better hold on your impulses, think of what you intend to do next and visualize that entire situation and process. For instance, if you are going to order a salad, imagine calling a healthy food eatery and placing an order for a big salad bowl. As a treat, you could opt for your favorite dressing even if it has some extra calories than what you should have. Imagine receiving your order in the lead time mentioned by the eatery and getting it on time. Picture yourself enjoying your meal and having a great time with it. Describe the scenario below, and then practically execute it.
- If you aren't experiencing any impulsive urges right now, think of a time when you displayed strong impulsive

behavior. What was it, and how did you react in that situation?

- If you gave into that impulse at that point, what made you do so? For instance, if you made a big purchase worth $1,000, why did it happen?
- Think of how you could have avoided that impulsive behavior, and picture yourself engaging in that practice. If you engaged in some meaningless shopping, you could have avoided it by shutting down your laptop if you were shopping online or going for a walk. Imagine doing these things right now in that scenario.
- Now write down how you feel about yourself and how you plan to function in a situation where your feel like behaving impulsively.

Keep these tactics in mind and observe them every time you experience an urge to do something impulsively.

Exercise for Emotional Control

Here is a **set of tasks** that promotes better emotional control.

- Think of any emotion you have been experiencing intensely lately or an emotion that's interfering with your routine tasks. Try to name that emotion specifically and describe how it makes you feel.
- If thinking about it upsets you, practice the deep breathing technique. This technique will come in handy throughout this journey of empowering your self-control, so practice it as often as possible. I will share a couple of other breathing exercises in the last part of the book too, but for now, stick to this one because it is super-effective

and straightforward to practice for anyone, even novices.
- Now take a moment to think of how that emotion is disrupting your life or how it keeps causing you to react impulsively and give up on things you want to do. Jot down your feelings here. You can later write them down in another journal, but using this space ensures you don't forget or miss out on any information and solidify them quickly.
- Close your eyes and think of how your life would look if you took control of this particular emotion and trained yourself to tone it down. Once again, note down your thoughts here.
- Now think of the emotion you want to feel and the reason behind it. For example, if you feel weak, but want to feel confident, imagine what confidence feels like to you and how you would feel being confident. Express your feelings here.
- Now imagine tackling that situation from the perspective of the new emotion you want to experience, then describe your feelings here.

Every time you feel like an emotional wreck, carry out this practice, and you will easily tackle the situation with your emotions in check, thereby making the best decision possible.

Exercise for Movement Control

As you work on the exercises above, you automatically gain better movement control. To improve it, try this exercise:

- Think of the last time you were in a situation where you did not manage your bodily movements well, or

perhaps a situation where you acted in a disruptive manner. Describe it here.
- What do you think made you react in that manner? And why did it happen?
- How do you think you could have controlled the problem better?
- Now replay the entire episode in your head again, and picture yourself handling yourself and the situation confidently and sensibly. What do you see yourself doing differently now?

Work on this exercise a couple of times every week, and soon you will have better control over your disruptive and unexpected bodily reactions and gestures.

Exercise for Concentration Control

People usually struggle the most with developing concentration control. The primary reason for this is that we have somehow built the habit of doing several things at once, which divides our attention.

As you are reading this book, you may be thinking about what to wear to work tomorrow, checking up on your email, and maybe doing a couple of other tasks in between, too, all at the same time. As astounding as it sounds, in reality, this practice only disrupts our sense of focus and promotes mental chaos.

We are not designed to focus on multiple things at once. That is why we experience constant headaches and concentration issues because we force ourselves to do something we are not designed to do.

As difficult as it seems to develop concentration control, developing it is not that tough. With some practice and a lot of consistency, you can easily master it.

Here is a very simple exercise to get you started, and of course, if you have been working on the exercises discussed above, you will find this one even easier to execute.

- While reading this book right now, just point out one thought that you keep having time and again, or any other task that you are also doing meanwhile. Perhaps you are scrolling through your social media feed or organizing clothes in your drawer. Whatever you are doing, please write it down here.
- While being honest to yourself, consider and answer how undivided your attention is at the moment and how it is keeping you from focusing on just reading the book. Write your thoughts about this below:
- Next, say, 'I am reading this book with complete focus and take a deep breath. Carry out this practice about five times, and write down how you feel.
- Gently fixate your attention on the book only, and every time you wander off in thought, take a deep breath and calmly realign your attention to the book. Write down how many times you had to engage in this practice before you started fully focusing on reading the book.
- Also, write down how you felt if you could read the book even for 5 minutes with complete focus. You may realize that you read more pages or understood even one page better than when reading it with divided attention. Express your feelings here.

Every time you carry out any task, carry out this practice before getting started and then start it off. The more you practice this, the better you will get at fully concentrating on one task at a time, and the faster you shall build your concentration control.

Now that you are well aware of the kinds of self-control and how to start working on developing each type, let us talk about how self-control affects the pursuit and fulfillment of your goals in the next chapter.

"When we are sure that we are on the right road there is no need to plan our journey too far ahead. No need to burden ourselves with doubts and fears as to the obstacles that may bar our progress. We cannot take more than one step at a time."

—Orison Swett Marden

PART 3

SELF-CONTROL AND GOAL ACHIEVEMENT

> *"You cannot prevent the birds of sorrow from flying over your head, but you can prevent them from building nests in your hair."*
>
> —Chinese proverb

This proverb is the perfect example of how empowered you become when you build and improves your self-control. You may not have the power to control the onset of different challenges in your life, but you can most definitely control for how long they affect you and continue to ruin your life.

Setbacks, obstacles, and challenges are a part of everyone's life. Only those who combat and defeat Setbacks, obstacles, and challenges emerge victorious in life. We set many goals right, but for some reason, try as we may, many of those goals remain elusive and out of reach. These stretch goals, as many people so often call them, aren't impossible to achieve. It is just that they lie outside our comfort zone and constantly test our resolve and ability to move outside our comfort zones.

That is where self-control comes in to help you accomplish the impossible.

The Role of Self-Control in Achieving Our Goals

Chasing any goal, especially one that tests your limits, is not easy. It demands motivation, knowledge, skills, resources, inspiration, and self-discipline. But most of all, it demands that you be in control of yourself. It is mostly in this very area that many of us fall short and end up quitting our goals.

Often, we have this ideal vision of how our goal will look like at a point in life. That said, moving from where we currently are to that desired point requires us to take numerous steps, many of which feel overwhelming and daunting. Progression through these milestones is certainly doable, but it asks us to invest in focused effort and self-control.

Most people falter at this point: taking consistent steps with self-control does not come naturally to many of us, so we don't get the desired results. We can achieve some progress, but it is often sporadic and conflicts with our desires. That happens due to a lack of self-control. That is why it is pre-emptive to work on your self-control before embarking on a journey to actualize a goal.

How self-control comes into play?

Self-control is more like a routine where you choose to focus on your long-term goals and adopt a sincere attitude towards them. You think rationally about what you want, which is why you can successfully stay focused on the bigger picture.

Practicing self-control allows you to override unwanted feelings, impulses, habits, and thoughts because self-control builds on a foundation of intrinsic motivation.

Intrinsic motivation refers to behavior driven by different internal rewards. It is a behavior you perceive as naturally pleasurable and satisfying. Instead of looking for extrinsic rewards such as monetary gains, material wins, and fancy objects, you seek rewards that come from within you.

Let us elaborate on this.

Extrinsic and Intrinsic Motivation

Intrinsic motivation comes from internal elements; on the other hand, extrinsic motivation, as the name suggests, arises from external factors.

Being intrinsically motivated means that you engage in

activities solely because they mean a lot to you and because you enjoy them and derive personal satisfaction from them. You find those activities satisfying, meaningful, and rewarding. The goals tied to your intrinsic motivation come from within, and their outcomes quench your thirst for the basic psychological need for relatedness, competence, and autonomy.

On the other hand, being extrinsically motivated means that you engage in an activity to attain an external reward. Such activities do not satisfy your basic psychological needs but relate to external gains like fame, power, money, or avoiding consequences.

Your self-control associates with your intrinsic motivation, consequently helping you achieve your most meaningful goals.

Self-Control and Intrinsic Motivation: The Connection Between the Two

Think of any monumental goal you have ever achieved in life, or if you are yet to accomplish one, think of the one you desperately want to materialize. It could be the time you worked out regularly to lose 30 pounds, or when you set up your first online firm, or when you graduated from college without financial assistance from anyone.

Whatever that goal was or is, it certainly matters to you a lot. If you dig deeper into it, you will realize that it holds a special place in your life because it pertains to your core values. What are core values, you may ask? Core values are the beliefs you hold on to very dearly and use to live your life a certain way. They are your most important principles, and knowingly or unknowingly, you use them to shape your life a certain way.

When you feel driven to accomplish a goal, it's because

it coincides with your core principles. Sticking to your values and materializing them is a form of intrinsic motivation. You feel alive doing something that pertains to what you genuinely care about and what you feel you cannot live without for one or another reason.

This brings you a sense of fulfillment and pleasure because you see yourself striving for what you believe in and giving it a shape of reality. When there is a congruence between your values and what you achieve, you feel intrinsically motivated.

Where does self-control fit in this entire scenario?

Well, by now, you are aware that change is the only constant thing in our lives. No matter how prepared you are for a journey, some challenge will come your way. In such scenarios, our motivation often runs low, making us tremble and question the pursuit of our goals. However, this does not remain the case when you practice self-control.

In the presence of self-control, you keep revisiting your core values and principles. You keep reflecting on what matters most to you, and this constant reminiscence motivates you to push yourself forward in times of adversity. What you value is what you truly desire, and that propels you towards the finish line. That is how you eventually reach your desired destination.

Your intrinsic motivation becomes a source of self-control. It reminds you of what you are passionate about and what you must not give up on at any cost, so you strive for what genuinely matters to you and achieve your goal.

Now that you understand how self-control relates to goal achievement, let me give you some tactics you can use.

Know your core values

First things first:

If you aren't yet aware of your core values, it is time to bring them to the surface. It is not like you don't have core values; the only thing is that you are not consciously aware of them yet.

All of us have values and principles we use to structure our lives. Quite often, we aren't aware of those values, and so we don't use them to our advantage to build self-control.

To take charge of your life and practice self-restraint whenever you need and want to, you must be conscious of your core values. Being value-conscious helps you figure out the factors that shape your intrinsic motivation, thereby allowing you to leverage them to advance towards your goal.

Here's how you can figure out your core principles:

- Take your journal or recorder and sit somewhere calm.
- Dedicate some time to reflecting on the guiding principles you have always held dear to your heart or the ones you have always believed in for this or that reason. They may not be the values you are currently following. For instance, honesty may have been dear to you once, but recently, you may have ditched it many times to achieve some ulterior motives you wrongfully believed were part of your goals. What have you always believed in or want to believe in now? You can jot it down here or record yourself talking about it.
- Think of the current state of your life, and describe it as you feel it. For example, if you feel that your current life is chaotic, unstructured, and does not bring you joy, write it down. Ensure you also explain why you feel that way.

- Reflect on the core values that contribute to the current state of your life. If your life lacks structure, it could be because you don't sleep and rise early, which likely stems from your core value of not following any structure and routine in your life. Discuss those principles here.
- Close your eyes and imagine yourself following your core values. Describe what you see and how that makes you feel here.
- Lastly, create a simple positive affirmation that makes you feel as if you are following your core values, so you start to abide by them regularly. Positive affirmations are positive suggestions you believe to be truthful, so you start following them religiously.

  The more you practice them, the better they become a part of your subconscious mind, and once something becomes part of your subconscious, it starts to rewire your mind to think more in that direction. By chanting a positive affirmation centered on your core value, you tell yourself that you already follow that value, ensuring that your subconscious mind accepts it.

  As a result, it becomes a part of your belief system and shapes your life in real. If integrity is your core value, you could say, 'I value integrity and use it to live an honest life.' Go ahead and create a positive affirmation on any of your most significant core values. It should be positive, crisp, concise, and make you feel like you already practice it. Journal it down below.
- After writing it, say it aloud about ten times or more times until you start to believe it.
- In addition, spend some of your daily time thinking about what interests, inspires, moves, and excites you.

This way, you will understand the core values you want to believe in. Also, read up on different topics, subjects, and areas of life to expose yourself to more knowledge, and set core values you genuinely want to believe in and follow.

Carry out this practice or about ten times daily until you get clarity on your core values. Practice it even after that to ensure you keep your core values in mind and sight and use them religiously to structure your desired reality.

Identify Your Intrinsic Motivators

Once you know what your core values are, finding your intrinsic motivators becomes relatively easier. Intrinsic motivators are all the factors and elements you seek as you set and achieve a goal. You can also refer to them as your reasons for wanting to achieve a goal or something else.

Goals share a bond with the motivation that comes from knowing that a goal has a reward pegged to it. For example, you know losing weight will help you get a slender body, help you become healthier, and help you control your diabetes, so you become motivated to achieve the goal of losing weight, right?

In this very manner, every goal provides you with some rewards that motivate you to pursue it. These rewards are the reasons, aka the compelling whys that excite you for that goal and shape your intrinsic motivation.

To know why you need to set a goal and materialize it, you must discover your intrinsic motivators. Now that you know your core values, doing so isn't going to be much of a hassle.

Here's what you should do:

- Take your most important core value and think of how it makes your life better. If 'autonomy' is one of your core values, think of how it makes you free and gives you the freedom to live life on your terms. Describe that in your words and write it here.
- Now imagine yourself using that core value to live a better life or the life you desire. Continuing with the example of the core value of 'autonomy,' think of how autonomous you will feel when you move off your blood pressure drugs and live a life characterized by freedom. Think about a time when you are so physically and mentally fit that you have the reins of your life in your own hands. Similarly, think of how your chosen core value can help improve the quality of life and write about it here.
- Next, reflect on your ideal life, what it looks and feels like, and what you see yourself doing while living this life. Write about it below:
- After that, think of what you can do to achieve that state of life and how you can use your chosen core values to your advantage. Explain your sentiments in the workspace below.
- Why do you think you must not make do without your core values, principles, and your ideal life?
- Reflect on the little accounts you have just written. These are all your intrinsic motivators; they are the reasons why you need to build self-control.

Now let's go a step further and tie them all to a goal to have even more clarity on your compelling whys.

Know What Particular Goal to Achieve

Let us further build on your intrinsic motivators and figure out exactly what goal you wish to achieve. It becomes easier to exercise self-control when you know what all that effort leads to at the end of it all.

When you know how working 10 hours, sacrificing your time out with friends and family, saving money to start a business, and spending time learning new skills will help you achieve what you want to achieve, you become motivated to do so.

That is why you must know what you are trying to achieve, so you become clear and focused on it and invest your efforts in the right direction.

- Go through all your core values, ideal life, and compelling whys, and try to find a connection amongst all these factors. What does all of that allude to, or what does it tell you instinctually? Write that down here.
- Now think about how your talents, skills, and strengths relate to the discovery you have made above. Here, you need to find a point where everything you are excited about, good at, and feel strongly about converge. This converging point will help you explore and identify your goal.
- Also, list down some of the most important areas of your life. First, write down the different areas of your life such as health, nutrition, fitness, religion, science, family, friends, work, wealth, etc. Now, rank them in order of importance. Use the space below to do it easily now.
- Pick the three most important ones, and analyze them in the light of your core values, strengths, skills, and

dream life. What can you do to improve those areas using your core values?

Take an instance where your health, wealth, and career matter the most to you. Equally, your core values are sincerity, passion, and adventure, and you are good at fitness and training individuals, and you want to live an independent life without the fear of your paycheck getting too late. In that case, you could start a fitness center.

You are passionate about staying fit and inspiring others to be the same. Instructing and training others is what you are good at, so it coincides with your strength. You will get to be your own boss and slowly grow your business so you can stop living from one paycheck to another. That will be an exciting journey, so the element of 'adventure' will be pretty much present in it.

If you analyze this entire scenario, you can see how this goal pertains to all the discoveries you have made throughout this time and is a sum of what you genuinely aspire to do. With this, you can create a specific goal that aligns with what you believe in, a goal that inspires you to be better by the day. With your aspirations, strengths, core principles, and ambitions in mind, determine a specific goal that you wish to achieve and describe it here.

After getting clearer on your goal, think of what having self-control means in light of your goal.

What Will it Mean to Have Self-Control?

As you already know, self-control means having a better grip on your temptations, so you do what's right and expected of you instead of what you feel tempted to do at a specific time. With your precise goal in front of you, you now need to deeply understand what having self-control would mean to you and what it would look like in practice.

- Write down what you wish to achieve. For example, "I want to start a fitness center and make it the best one in the city."
- Reflect on what that goal would require you to do and the kind of person you would have to become to achieve the goal.

Continuing with the example mentioned above, if you want to start a fitness-based facility, you need to have a physically fit body, so people know you practice what you preach.

Secondly, you would need to discipline your life and have a routine to create some room for your business in it. Thirdly, you would need to work long hours—at least at the start. You may also need funds for it, and perhaps a certification in the field of health and fitness. You are likely to require more things too, but for now, let us stick with these. Use this example to figure out what your goal demands from you, the journal the experience below:

- Next, think of what temptations you will have to control and the different ways you will need to exercise self-restraint if you are to fulfill all these obligations you are likely to have towards your goal. For example, to become physically fit and athletic, you need to have a balanced diet with increased protein intake, work out more, and have a strict fitness regimen.

  To execute all of that, you will have to give up on

sleeping in daily. You will also need to cut back on your consumption of sweets, and you will need to focus more on having home-cooked meals. These are all the ways you will have to practice self-control.

Consider your goal now and explore how you will have to control your urges to fulfill it.

- Take your time to list down all things you need to practice self-control on concerning your goal. Go through the list a couple of times, revise it if needed, and re-write the list on a fresh leaf in your journal.

Now you have in front of you a list of all the things you need to exercise self-control on to achieve your respective goal. There is no other way about it. To accomplish your desired feat, you need to work on the respective areas. That means you will have to give up instant gratification and be ready to burn the midnight oil, go the extra mile and pursue delayed gratification.

I know you understand immediate gratification and the importance of beating it to achieve your goals, but let us get into its details to understand it better.

PART 4

IMMEDIATE GRATIFICATION AND
BEATING TEMPTATION

'The ability to discipline yourself to delay gratification in the short term in order to enjoy greater rewards in the long-term is the indispensable pre-requisite for success.'

—Brian Tracy

Delayed gratification is what leads to the desired and truly profitable outcomes. Unless you prioritize it over immediate gratification, you won't move towards your ideal life. This realization may sound harsh right now, but time will help you realize that this is the ultimate truth.

Now you are aware of the definition of immediate gratification and how it holds you back. Let's build on this knowledge and discuss the strategies you can employ to spot it timely and ultimately beat temptations to achieve what you deserve.

Symptoms of Instant Gratification

To beat the urge to pursue instant gratification and succumb to your temptations, you should first figure out whether or not you engage in that.

Here are the symptoms you need to look out for in yourself for 5 to 7 days to be sure of whether or not you practice instant gratification every time you set out on a journey.

- **Act impulsively:** You don't take the time to think things through; instead, you act impulsively, especially whenever you encounter a situation.
- **Get stuck in problems:** Since you cannot stop acting impulsively, you often find yourself stuck in dilemmas.
- **Feel unsatisfied:** No matter what you do or achieve, you never feel satisfied because your hungry beast always wants more in life. Moreover, since you always opt for immediate gratification, you never really get what you genuinely want.

This dilemma leaves you feeling unsatisfied and unfulfilled.
- **Cannot control the behaviors you wish to control:** You want to leash certain behaviors, but since most of them happen impulsively, you cannot control them timely.
- **Lack of patience:** Often, you don't act patiently. Instead, you react impatiently, don't wait for things to settle down or give yourself time to assess a situation to respond better, and jump the gun. That is why you keep yourself from attaining what you genuinely deserve.
- **Never master anything:** You often jump from one branch to another. In real life, you do that with the goals and activities you engage in daily. You constantly leap from one goal to another, one skill to another, and one activity to another keeps you from mastering any area, skill, and activity. You hardly ever get anything done and struggle at becoming a pro at what you aspire.
- **Master self-gratification:** You do, however, master one thing: self-gratification. Instead of learning how to manage your temptations better so you can actualize your meaningful goals, you are busy fulfilling your short-term temptations.
- **Experience mood swings:** Every time you quit a task, you feel irritable, which leads to a bad mood swing. Even when you don't quit, you find yourself feeling cranky because of the constant feeling of being unsatisfied and unhappy with yourself.
- You often engage in whatever feels easier, convenient, and more pleasurable than your current activity.

After going through these symptoms, start observing yourself very keenly for a week. Because we tend to become biased towards ourselves and may ignore a certain sign even if it is visible to our naked eye, you can also ask a helpful friend to support you in this journey.

Our friends, on the other hand, aren't that biased. They are likely to call a spade a spade when they sense something. Asking a trustworthy and honest friend to help you means the person will tell you when they observe something wrong, which will help you identify the problem, and start the process of kicking the issue to the curb.

After tracking your behavior and symptoms with this table, you will have clarity on where you lie in terms of instant gratification. Now that you know where you stand and how frequently you opt for immediate gratification, let us walk through the different reasons we fall for instant gratification.

Reasons That Compel Us to Give into Instant Gratification

Although many reasons compel you to give in to your temptations, primarily, most of us are likely to surrender to our whims due to the following reasons:

Emotional gratification: This is quite a massive problem for many of us. Human beings are emotional creatures that quite often react impulsively to emotions. Your emotions kick in when you see a certain temptation, and before you realize it, it has lured you in.

For example, you may feel excited about seeing a clearance sale at a clothing store and rush to empty your wallets there. A few hours later, you realize how the sale didn't do you much good but only cash strapped you until your next paycheck.

Lack of patience: The absence of patience is an enormous problem that often obstructs the path towards your goals.

Besides being a symptom of pursuing immediate gratification, a lack of patience is also why you keep quitting your meaningful pursuits halfway through.

Sense of entitlement: Having a sense of entitlement means you strongly believe you deserve something right now and must not wait for it, or else somebody else may get it first. This urges you to go for that thing right now before it gets too late. Also, you believe that only you have the right over that thing, which further compels you to pursue it.

Lack of trust in your abilities: Low sense of self-esteem makes you question your abilities and strengths. Instead of exploring your potential and honing it, you end up doubting it. Quite likely, when you disregard your abilities, you don't see yourself making it to the finish line.

Doubts, fears, and insecurities orbit your mind, further straining your self-confidence. In such times, you find it easier to give in to your temptations and allow them to sidetrack you. As a result, you quit your goals and embrace immediate gratification.

Scarcity mindset: The scarcity mindset refers to thinking that things are limited in quantity. Quite often, this is where immediate gratification stems from. You feel there aren't enough things in the world for you to enjoy, and it is quite likely what you want now may be finished by the time you reach for it. Following these thoughts, you agree to oblige to your temptation and prioritize instant gratification.

Laziness: Being lazy is a significant reason why many of us fall short of sticking to a goal for the long haul and pursuing delayed gratification. Knowing that it will take you at least a decade to establish your business internationally means you will have to work quite hard for it.

Why work incredibly hard for something when the desired outcome is due in 10 years when you can get a decent compensation working for someone else now? Such thoughts keep you from being your own boss and find solace in working for someone else just because running a business on your own is more challenging.

This reason keeps you from setting and sticking to your goals quite often, and you keep giving them up for the sake of immediate gratification.

The process feels overwhelming: Trying to achieve a goal spread over a couple of weeks, let alone one spanning a few months, feels extremely overwhelming. Imagining doing lots of hard work, pulling all-niters, and sacrificing routine pleasures is not everyone's cup of tea. Naturally, in such scenarios, it feels more convenient to give in to instant gratification.

Lack of Vision: Vision refers to how you see your life panning out over a certain time. It is what you plan to attain over several years and how you wish to steer your life in a certain manner. If you compare those who accomplish their goals with those who only struggle to do so, you will realize that the former always have a vision for their lives; the latter don't have such a plan.

When you have a clear vision for yourself and your life, you know what you are trying to accomplish with a high degree of preciseness. That vision compels you to stay strong in the presence of adversities and not give in to your superficial desires.

In contrast, an absence of a vision keeps you from propelling yourself further in life. That's because you are unaware of what you aspire for in life. That is why you go for whatever catches your fancy and keep surrendering to your meaningless desires.

Being influenced by others: While we are accountable for our own lives, we cannot deny that people can have an influential power over us. Sometimes, it so happens that we make certain choices, even hasty ones, because of another peoples' influence.

For instance, you may be doing well on your fitness regimen and following the schedule daily. However, the day your old childhood friend shows up and convinces you to have a couple of drinks that soon lead to many bottles, your fitness regimen goes down the drain. It is not too bad if it is only an occasional occurrence. However, if that friend continues to influence you regularly, and you keep giving in to his requests, you are likely to forget all about your diet and fitness.

Likewise, other people in your life may convince you to give up certain goals or take routes that don't take you any closer to your objectives. The influences may not always be negative, but since they somewhat negatively influence you, let us refer to them as such.

If you have such influences in your life, that may be the reason why you get pulled towards your temptations quite often. What do the following have in common: Being asked by your co-worker to join you for a smoke, reminded by a cousin of your business failures, and encouraged by your spouse to ditch dieting and enjoy a juicy hamburger?

These are all examples of being swayed away from your commitments by different influences in your life. In such scenarios, it naturally becomes difficult to stick to what you believe. That is why it is crucial to cut ties with toxic influences, or at least learn how to manage them better if you cannot sever your bond with them right away.

Feeling overconfident: As important as it is to be self-confident, too much of this virtue can keep you from actualizing your goals. Sometimes, it so happens that overconfidence can get in the way of your dreams.

On achieving a milestone or two, you may find yourself becoming too self-absorbed, and that's when you allow your achievements to sway you away from the actual goal. Feeling in control of yourself, you may find it alright to give in to some temptations, and soon a few of them lead to many, and you become distracted from the real objective.

Just like you spent some time observing your behavior for the symptoms of seeking instant gratification, spend some more time reflecting on the core reasons behind this behavior. You may discover any of the reasons discussed above being the root cause of the problem.

Once you figure out the problem, it is time to fix the mess.

Replace Compulsive Urges with Alternative Behavior

A sure-fire hack to fix compulsive urges that drive you towards your temptations is to engage in alternative behaviors every time your temptations growl at you. It may seem difficult to do right now, but if you follow the step-by-step guidelines below, I assure you, it will be more of a piece of cake.

- First, figure out the compulsive behavior you are trying to overcome. In this case, you are working on seeking immediate gratification.
- Write down what you are trying to change. You could say, 'I am working on eliminating my behavior of giving in to instant gratification.'

- The trick to accomplishing a goal, especially that of beating a bad habit, lies in being as specific as possible. The more specific you are, the better you understand the problem you are trying to overcome. Here, this means you need to specifically point out the exact area you are trying not to act impulsively in. For instance, if you often spend heftily on sales, you could mention that specific instant gratification you are trying to overcome. If you seek instant gratification from eating high-calorie foods instead of eating healthy foods, mention that as the behavior you wish to improve. For example, you could say, 'I want to improve my resiliency to instant gratification when I diet to ensure that I eat healthier foods instead of unhealthy options.'
- Next, you need to start observing yourself very closely for that behavior. Can you remember the table I shared with you above? Create it once again, but this time, tweak it specifically for this impulsive behavior you are trying to change. Ensure you keep track of when you engage in it, why you do it, how it makes you feel, etc.
- Once you become more aware of how and when that happens, you understand its triggers and are more knowledgeable about how to control it in one way or another.
- Ensure that you pay attention to how it makes you feel to ensure that you can then search for an alternative behavior that offers the same or similar reward. An alternate is only viable when it stirs up similar feelings as the options you are replacing it for. For example, if you are training yourself not to give in to the urge to eat chocolate cake and eat some fruit instead, that

- is the substitute behavior you need to swap the initial behavior with.
- After deciding on the alternative behavior, you need to practice it every time you engage in the behavior you are trying to modify.
- It will feel slightly tough at first because you are not used to doing so, but soon you will get the hang of it. Make sure to be consistent with the practice because that's how you master it and learn the art of replacing temptation with an alternative behavior.

When you have a habit of chasing immediate gratification for a long time, delayed gratification feels like an old story of the past. Even with an alternate behavior in place, it can be difficult to exercise it sometimes. That's where the following hack comes in handy.

Say No to Yourself

Have you ever said no to your kid who kept asking for candy even when she has had her share for the day? Or the time when your dog kept jumping at you to play, but you knew he was over-excited and needed to sleep. As much as you wanted to agree to your loved one's wish, you still said no to them. Do you know why? That's because you care and know that refusing their demand was the right thing to do at that time.

The same rule applies to you right now. You need to start saying no to yourself every time temptations come rolling your way because that is the right thing to do.

Is it hard? Oh yes!

Is it doable? Absolutely!

Let me show you how:

- Start by taking a few deep breaths the instant you feel tempted to seek instant gratification. It calms you down, allowing you to think more rationally.
- Next, please think of the behavior you will engage in and how it is unfavorable for you.
- Write down those pointers on your journal or notepad on your mobile phone or make a mental note.
- Recall the alternative behavior you decided to engage in instead.
- Write that down or make a mental note of it along with the top 5 reasons why you should exercise it. For example, if you decided to drink cold water every time you feel like having a soda, write down why it is beneficial. For example, water keeps you hydrated. It is calorie-free, helps your brain function well, keeps you active, improves your skin, and so on.
- Go through these reasons at least thrice, so they start to sink deeper in your head.
- Now tell yourself the 'no' you need to tell yourself. 'No, I am going to drink water instead.' Make sure to say it out loudly and confidently to ensure that you believe it.
- Get up and do what you are chanting, so you take the step for real. Once you carry out the step, your temptation starts to fade away.

Start working on this idea, and soon you will start refusing your temptations in your sleep.)

Examine Your Feelings when You Give into a Temptation

Another pro tip you can use to manage instant gratification is to examine your feelings when temptations win you over.

Why do you need to do this? You need to do this because it will help you understand how giving into temptations may bring about temporary joy but lead to disappointment in the end. As you observe your feelings more often, you will know exactly how temptations make you feel and keep you from pursuing immediate gratification in the future.

- Let's say you have just missed a day's work on your blog because you wanted to sleep more, or perhaps binge-watch shows on Netflix. Whatever your temptation is, if you gave in to it, write it down.
- Write down what you did after paying heed to your temptation and if there were any consequences of it.
- Think of how those consequences messed up your life and kept you from achieving your desired reality.
- Weigh the weight of your temptation against the consequences, then rate both on a scale of 1 to 10, 10 being the highest.
- Write down that feeling and what giving in to your temptation costs you on a new page, have it printed, and put it up on your work desk or bedroom.
- Every time instant gratification tries to lure you, glance at that post-it, and you're likely not to pursue it.

As you exercise this tactic repeatedly, you become better at it and find it easier to practice it every time you feel weak in the knees with your temptation looming over and closing in on you.

List 10 Reasons Why Self-Control Matters

You need to practice self-control to ward off immediate gratification, right? However, you don't know why you should do so, do you? That is why you need to curate your ultimate list of all the reasons self-control matters.

- Take out your journal and think of 10 reasons why observing self-control can and should matter to you.
- Write them in bullets at first.
- Once done writing the ten reasons, elaborate on each.
- Also, write down how exactly each pointer adds value to your life.
- If you fall short of digging up ten reasons, think of all the times when your distractions weighed you down and got the better of you.
- Think of the things you missed out on because of your temptations.
- Soon, you'll have your list ready.

Make sure to reflect on it every day before hitting the bed so you become aware of what your self-control can do for you.

Reframe Impulsive Thoughts with Positive Affirmations

Impulsive thoughts tend to be quite sabotaging. However, how they impact you is entirely up to you. Instead of allowing those thoughts to ruin your life, why not get a better hold on them?

"How," you may ask? The answer is quite simple: you reframe them, harnessing the power of positive affirmations.

You already know what positive affirmations are. Now, you need to channelize their power one more time to reframe impulsive thoughts as you desire.

- Write down the impulsive thought you are having.
- For example, if your thought is, 'I want to sleep in more and not work,' write that down.
- Next, think of a positive substitute for this thought. How could you make it more positive and affirmative? Ask yourself this very question, and you will start getting positive answers.
- For instance, in this case, you need to think of why you must work and how it is important for you. You could say, 'I have to get up and work to achieve my professional goals/make more money.'
- Make sure the affirmation is concise, positive, and present-oriented; it suggests that you will do something.
- Chant it a couple of times, and soon enough, you will be distracted from the temptation.

As you practice a positive affirmation, ensure to get up and start working. The key to making all these tactics work is to get up and take the necessary action right away. There can be no other way about it. Unless you get up and do the actual task, the temptations are likely to bother you repeatedly.

Distract Yourself

All these tactics above are a means to distract yourself from your temptation. However, they make you focus on your goal—the bigger picture. Sometimes, you need a distraction to sidetrack yourself from another temptation because sometimes, zooming in on the bigger picture may overburden you.

In such scenarios, distract yourself from whatever captivates your attention and lures you from your actual goal by doing anything else. For example, if you are thinking of ordering a pizza while you are on a diet, go for a walk. If you want to binge-watch shows on Netflix, talk to an inspiring friend. For 5 minutes, turn your attention away from the temptation, and the chances are high that you won't return to it.

As I have said before, these hacks work if you are consistent with them, so start doing so, and you'll soon get a tight grip on your urge to pursue immediate gratification.

You now need to understand how willpower and self-control relate and the role of the two in empowering your self-control. Hover to the next chapter to find that out.

PART 5

SELF-DISCIPLINE AND WILLPOWER

*'Journey of a thousand miles
begins with a single step.'*

—Lao Tzu

Willpower, Self-Control, and Self Discipline

You cannot reach the finish line without running even for a bit.

You cannot set up a million-dollar empire overnight.

You cannot shed off 20 pounds in 2 days.

You cannot break your bad habit of procrastination in a couple of hours and get back on the right track.

Things don't work that way. We all wish they did, but the reality is that they don't and never will.

To complete the journey of a thousand miles, you have to take the first step forward, and that's how you propel yourself further towards your desired reality.

So far, we have learned the many ingredients you need to brew up success. Two terms often used a lot when you are trying to build your self-control are ***self-discipline*** and ***willpower***.

But what exactly is the difference between the two, and how are the two related? Also, how can you employ the two to develop and hone your self-control?

Let us first focus on the difference between the two, then strategies to help you master your self-control.

Willpower and self-control mean nearly the same thing. Both refer to controlling your impulses and temptations and the actions that follow once you pay heed to your impulses. When you practice self-control, you find yourself engaging in what's right and expected from you, not what catches your attention.

Willpower is more like the extent to which you can practice self-control. You may have noticed that you probably find it difficult to exercise for an hour if you have starved yourself throughout the day. Or that it becomes difficult to quit smoking, start exercising daily and work on learning a skill, all at the same time.

Trying to do too much at once depletes your willpower; it depletes your ability to practice self-control, and when it becomes hard to exercise self-control, you cannot get the desired results.

So how can one exercise self-control in the right manner?

What should you do to make sure you don't run low on your willpower?

How can you ascertain that you stay strong and confident at all times and make the right move always, or mostly at least?

That is where self-discipline comes into play.

Self-discipline, as you can see, is a noun that refers to disciplining yourself. If you are disciplining yourself, naturally, you are doing it for something. You can't just discipline yourself without having a set motive or without the desire to achieve something.

You want to discipline yourself to expand your willpower to practice self-control whenever required. You may be wondering why? So you keep taking one step after another and advance through that journey of a thousand miles.

When we talk about discipline, it is clear that it requires you to train yourself in a certain area. Training requires taking some real-time action. When you take some action, you become successful in going somewhere forward.

This training that you engage in must be daily-based because only consistent efforts yield compound results. Regular training helps you build self-control, which allows you to stay resolute on the right track and keep achieving one milestone after another.

So how does that distinguish self-discipline from willpower then?

The Difference Between Self-Discipline and Willpower

In his course titled, '*Choose to Win,*' Tom Ziglar talks about how self-discipline is the key to building and increasing your self-control, aka willpower.

Willpower, as I stated above, is the ability to stay steadfast on your journey. It is about digesting the urge to follow through with your temptations then deciding to do the right thing instead. It is about saying no to yourself every time you feel like staying idle, staying awake at night instead of hitting the bed on time, or procrastinating on your tasks. It's about saying no to an extra smoke, eating that juicy hamburger when you should have baked beans, and being firm with yourself every time your heart tries to flutter to the tune of a temptation.

On the other hand, self-discipline is about taking that course of action that enables you to say no to yourself and all your distractions each time they knock on your door.

It is about going to bed at 10 pm every night.

It is about exercising at 7 am every morning.

It is about having a diet of lean meat cuts, fresh greens, and whole wheat grains day in and day out.

It is about beating your distractions daily.

It is about doing everything you need to stay put and resolutely surpass different obstacles on your journey.

Let me explain that with an example.

Let us just say you have decided to wake up at 5 am every morning. To do that every day, you need to practice self-control.

Getting up at 5 am when the alarm beeps and fighting the urge to go back to sleep, especially when it feels the sweetest, is your ability to practice self-control. If you say no to yourself and get up, you are using your willpower to stay steadfast on the chosen journey.

To ensure that you always say no to your sleepy self every morning, you need to practice self-discipline. You have to create a routine comprised of a series of actions you partake in every single day.

In this scenario, you set up an alarm followed by several reminders on your phone to wake up. You can even put your alarm several feet away from you to push yourself to get up and turn it off. By the time you do so, you are already out of bed and awake. You could also sleep early daily to ensure you get 7 to 8 hours of sleep at night regularly and feel fresh when your alarm goes off in the morning.

These are some of the things you could do to discipline yourself. Doing that helps you inculcate self-discipline that consequently shapes your self-control. Hence, to beat temptations, you need self-control, and to structure it, you need to practice self-discipline.

Let us now focus on some strategies you can use to practice self-discipline and sustain your willpower.

Start by Working on One Habit at a Time

Your willpower drains out fast when you overburden yourself. There is no rat race that you need to follow through or a competition you need to win. Nobody is going to give you a medal for overcoming ten unhealthy habits at once. Why not go on your pace then?

Slow and steady wins the race; make it your motto when it comes to building self-control.

- Go through the list of your most important goals, or the areas you wish to improve, those that you identified earlier.
- Identify a couple of habits in each area that holds you back. It could be procrastination, smoking, not working out, sleeping late, etc.
- Pick one that impacts your well-being and productivity the most or one that you want to overcome first.
- Stick to working on it for a couple of weeks or until you feel ready to work on the next thing in line.

Visualize Yourself Exercising Self-Control

After deciding which area, you need to work on first, carry out a quick exercise to rewire your mind to think positively and fuel your willpower. You need to believe you are capable enough to take charge of your situation and achieve the goal you have just set above.

Visualization is a sure-fire way to do so. It uses imagery to help you believe what you want to accomplish. The subconscious mind accepts whatever you feed it. If you repeatedly tell yourself how you are unsuccessful or doomed in life, it believes that. That is why you feel incompetent and never work hard enough to achieve your goals.

Now that you have committed to living a better life, let us try a different approach: making yourself believe you can do everything right.

- Close your eyes, and picture yourself engaging in the unhealthy behavior you want to improve. For instance, if you procrastinate a lot, especially when it comes to hitting the gym, imagine yourself not getting up right at 4 pm—or your set time to work out.
- As you build on the scenario, visualize yourself getting up, chanting a positive affirmation such as, 'I intend to work out and enjoy it so much,' so you feel the positive energy of the suggestion run in your body.
- After getting up, envision yourself doing your designed workout or hitting the gym.
- Imagine moving from one exercise to another very smoothly, doing the sets and rounds successfully, and enjoying the workout with each passing minute.
- Feel free to fill in details such as sights, colors, sounds, expressions, and emotions to the visualization to make it feel alive to you. The more it feels alive, the deeper you engage in it.
- After playing that video in your head for a good 5 to 10 minutes, gently stop it. At this point, you should be done with your imaginary workout and feel more in control of yourself.

Practice this exercise a couple of times during the day, even if you are not working on that respective habit. It activates your RAS, the reticular activating system, a system in your brain that filters out unnecessary information from the essential bits, ensuring that you focus on what matters. Once it is active, you focus better on that respective information, habit, or practice.

Identify your Triggers and Distractions

Your willpower grows when you know what you need to overcome. It is difficult to control your thoughts and emotions and work on eliminating a bad habit when you don't know what exactly triggers it. For example, you may continue to give in to your bad habit of procrastination if you are unaware that being overwhelmed or completing difficult tasks triggers and aggravates it.

Considering that, it is crucial to figure out the triggers of the respective bad habit you are trying to break and the distractions that ambush you and aggravate the matter.

- Write down the habit you are trying to beat.
- Now think of the different times, one at a time, when you have engaged in it.
- If you are thinking about procrastinating, think of what scenarios you procrastinate in and what exactly triggers this urge every time.
- Note down those different areas and situations. There could be multiple reasons or just one. It could be because a certain task is difficult, or because you don't feel passionate about doing it, or don't have the required skill set to work on it effectively. Whatever they are, try to delve deeper into them.
- Also, ponder on what distracts you from working on that respective issue. For example, if you are trying to overcome procrastination, why do you fail to do so every time? What sidetracks you? What is it that takes away your attention from it? These are all the distractions you need to work on, one at a time.

Having this information helps you know the obstacles that obstruct your path and eat away at your willpower. Now your job is to use this knowledge to create a foolproof plan to beat the issues.

Plan How to Build Self-Discipline

Planning is a good strategy to reduce the likelihood of setbacks and failures. It is similar to having a roadmap to follow when traveling. With your itinerary, you know where your stops are, what sights to see next, and when to get back on the road to ensure seamless movement from one place to the other.

This is also similar to switching on the GPS when finding a new location. You don't want to get lost, so you take the necessary help in the form of an already set route you could follow.

Similarly, when working on your self-control, you don't want to feel lost. You don't want to keep losing your grip on your willpower. You don't want to give in to your temptations frequently. You don't want to lose sight of the bigger picture.

You want results.
You want growth.
You want prosperity.
You want to live your life on your terms.
You want to feel disciplined.

Since that's the case, let us get straight to planning for it in the best way possible:

Think of a reasonable time to work on your bad habit. If you are trying to overcome procrastination, and have struggled with it for years now, give yourself at least six months to successfully defeat it. On average, it takes anywhere from 21 to 90 days to break a bad habit and stick to the new, healthier one, so at least give yourself 90 days, if not more.

Turn your goal into a SMART goal. That means it needs to be specific, measurable, attainable, realistic, and time-tagged. Smart goals ensure that you know exactly what to do, how to measure your pressure, how to get started with, how to follow through with it, and the timeframe to complete it.

A *specific* goal is one that clearly states what you wish to do without any room for ambiguity. If you are working on overcoming procrastination, specify the area or activity. For instance, do you procrastinate when it comes to exercising, making home-cooked meals, work-related chores, going to couples therapy, exactly what? If you are generally a procrastinator in every area of your life, just write down that.

Measurable goals specify the approach you take to gauge your performance in that area. To know whether or not you are doing well in a respective area, you will have to track your performance in that area. You cannot do that unless you have a measurable way of doing so. For instance, to see whether or not you are overcoming the urge to procrastinate, check your workplace productivity or the number of hours you work every day.

Next, make your goal *attainable* by figuring out the current resources you have to work on it. It would be incredible if all of us could have access to infinite money, skills, time, and every other imaginable resource we need to achieve our goal, but reality doesn't work that way.

That said, this does not mean you cannot get started with a certain goal right away with what you have right now. You can do so easily because even when you think you have nothing at your disposal, you still have a handful of resources you can easily exploit. Considering your goal, think of the available resources you can take advantage of right now.

In the example of procrastination, you can ask a friend to motivate you. You could also set reminders to work, change your environment positively, and you could learn the skills to do well in your work, so you stop feeling incompetent.

Fourthly, the goal should also be ***realistic,*** which means it should come off as believable. Hey, nobody is stopping you from believing in yourself and dreaming as big as possible; please, do that always.

Having said that, if you instantly set a goal to workout daily for 2 hours a day when you haven't worked out in 10 years, not only will it sound unrealistic to you, but it may also hurt your body when you try to push yourself too hard after a long hiatus.

The solution: set a simple, clear goal that sounds believable enough to you.

Lastly, peg it to a starting and ending date to ensure you know when to start working on it and its due date. Having this is crucial; otherwise, the chances are high that you may postpone your goal and forget all about it. However, these two dates need to be flexible enough to ensure that you can easily embark on this journey and complete a goal on time.

For instance, you could say, 'I will start to beat procrastination from 1st August and overcome it by 31st October 2021 to increase my productivity.'

Once you have turned your goal into a SMART one, chop it down into smaller bits and pieces. Spread it across six or more months, so it feels accommodating enough, but it also feels overwhelming when a goal spans over even a couple of months. Ditch this bit by chopping it down into smaller chunks that feel more doable to you.

For example, you can break down a six-month goal into either six milestones of one month each, or three milestones of two months, or any way that feels easier and viable to you. There is no hard and fast rule to planning your goal because all of us are different; we set different goals and work on them differently.

Go through the list of your distractions and temptations and find actionable strategies to beat them. If you procrastinate when a friend shows up, stop meeting him. If you smoke with your coworkers, stop spending time with them.

In addition, take some time to think of the habit you want to build in its place. What is it that you want to replace procrastination? Do you want to take intentional action in its place? Do you want to start going for a walk? What is it that you wish to do?

You need to work on it slowly to turn it into a habit. For instance, if you smoke, perhaps you can use nicotine patches in the start to break the bad habit, and also drink water, go for a walk, or dance when you experience a strong impulse to smoke. How can you best identify which practice to replace a certain behavior or habit with? I'll discuss this in the next pointer.

For now, let's get back to planning for the habit change. So, let's assume you have figured out the habit you want to bring in place of the existing one to build self-control.

With that figured out, create a schedule for when to and how to engage in it, accompanied by fixed alarms and reminders. For instance, you decide to work out daily for 15 minutes to kill your habit of procrastination, what time do you intend to do so, where do you want to work out, and what workout routine are you going to follow? Clarity on these aspects ensures you are well prepared to work out right on time.

Now, think of the different activities you need to engage in it to bring it about. The habit change you want to bring about and the one or a couple of behaviors you are trying to adopt in exchange are a few of the activities you need to engage in to achieve your respective goal.

Think about the other things required to accomplish that feat. For example, if you are trying to discipline yourself to learn digital skills to build your profile and find better freelance clients, you don't just have to learn the skill(s) you have chosen. You also need to create your profile on social media platforms, build your presence on freelance marketplaces, actively bid on projects, create gigs, network around, and spread the word about your work.

The work required to do is not just limited to only these activities. You would also need to sleep well, document your journey, track your performance, and eliminate any other bad habits that keep you from meeting your targets.

Identify all these key areas, write down what you need to do, then connect the dots to create a schedule you can work with daily. Every day, you need to engage in about 3 to 5 high-priority tasks pertinent to your goal; that way, instead of staying stagnant or floating on the same spot, you swim further.

Go through your schedule, dedicate a fixed time for every activity, and start engaging in it to achieve your goals. Now let us talk a little about how you can find the right substitutes for the habits you are trying to break.

What are the rewards attached to them? Start asking yourself these powerful questions to get powerful answers in return.

- Write down those rewards.
- Contemplate whether or not you get the same reward from the respective habit every time and express your sentiments on how it makes you feel.
- These are the gains you have to look for in a substitute behavior. For example, if smoking relaxes you, comforts you, and provides you with entertainment, you need to replace it with a practice that does the same for you.
- The tricky thing about habit change is that it is tough to find just one habit that serves as the perfect alternative for an existing habit, especially if you have grown addicted to the current practice. When I say addiction, I am not just talking about smoking or drinking alcohol; addiction can be anything, even procrastination.
- The key to doing this right is to create a combination of different practices, each of which provides one or more than one of the gains you seek from the unhealthy habit you are trying to break. Brainstorm some practices, activities, and behaviors that seem enticing to you, and those you suspect would provide you with the same rewards.
- Make a list of those. You could put meditation, jogging, cycling, dancing, painting, watching comedy videos, reading comic strips, having a film night with friends, and similar activities on the list to break the said bad habit.
- Ensure that you also note down some activities that improve your productivity and relate directly to your

desired goal. For instance, if you are training yourself to write a book of around 500 pages, one of the practices you could build is to write two pages daily. To feel inspired to write and overcome writer's block, you can read different books, spend time in nature, take a Zumba class, etc. Such activities keep you entertained and mitigate stress while also improving your productivity at the same time.

- Now comes the actual part of execution: you need to pick any one of the mentioned activities and carry it out for real. See whether or not it provides you the expected return. If it doesn't, cross it off the list. If it offers even 10% of the potential reward, keep it on the list.
- Engage in different activities in this manner, and once you have experimented with a couple, if not a handful, pick the most effective ones, and use them to build your creative mix. That is the mix you are now going to follow.
- To follow the strategy to ensure it gives you the desired results, you should also create a schedule. Set a time of the day and a fixed duration for every activity, considering how powerful it is in controlling your urges. Every time you experience a relatively low to mild temptation, engage in the least influential practice- one that curbs the temptation and gets you back on track. Keep the most powerful ones for times when your willpower runs sparingly low.
- Start working on the schedule and keep track of the results.

To get the most out of this routine, be mindful of yourself and your emotions during the drill. You need to know when a certain temptation compels you to hit rock bottom, so you curb it before it drives you insane.

Manage Your Emotions

As you work on building self-discipline, it is paramount to keep your emotions in check. We are emotional beings. We follow this rule to the T to the extent that we blame most of our hasty decisions and shortcomings on our emotions. We forget that we are also intellectual beings with incredibly powerful brains.

Yes, our emotions can at times screw us, but even that power lies within our control. On average, emotion shouldn't mess up with your rational thinking power for more than 12 minutes, say 15 at the most. Even then, we carry a lifelong relationship with anger, envy, sadness, fear, frustration, and what not, for years.

Do you know why this is the case? It's because you don't let go of those emotions. Let us focus on how to befriend your emotions instead of letting them become your boss. This way, you use them to your advantage without shunning them. Plus, you get back on the driver's seat, making sure you say no to your temptations every time they come to blow off your plans.

- Start observing your emotions with mindfulness. While this involves a lot of self-observation that may feel a tad bit annoying, trust the process. Awareness is the key to knowing yourself better and using your emotions, thoughts, weaknesses, and internal assets to your advantage.
- As you observe your emotions, notice how specific emotions make you give in to certain temptations.

Perhaps, you are going strong on your diet plan but give in to the urge of eating an ice cream sundae the day you reach 25,000+ followers on Instagram. Maybe, you have been off cigarettes for two weeks now, but one huge fight with your girlfriend and you puff off a whole pack of smokes.

- It is okay to give in to these urges. It happens, so don't beat yourself up too much about it. However, what's not okay is if you don't learn from the experiences.
- Make keen observations, write them down, and stay on the lookout for those emotions the next time.
- When you sense them building up, quickly distract yourself and excuse yourself from that very situation and location. Here's a scenario that will explain this better for you to understand. Let's say you are just about to reach 35,000 Instagram followers and become an even bigger influencer than before. Recall what happened the time you hit 25,000 followers. Before you get the notification of hitting the thirty-fifth thousandth follower, go out for a run, drink some water, shut down your laptop, or do anything that keeps you from being ecstatic to the extent that you again breach your diet plan.
- As you get a little distracted from that overwhelming emotion, take deep breaths. Take about 5 to 10, and you'll feel calmer than before.
- Deep breathing circulates more oxygen in your blood, which activates the parasympathetic response in the body to help you relax. When you feel calmer, you think better, which helps counteract the impulsive response you are likely to have all this time.
- The next thing is to think of what the emotion is

trying to teach you. Whether it is anger, joy, surprise, envy, greed, or fear, every emotion is trying to give you some valuable insight about yourself and your ability to exercise willpower. Understand that insight, and you will fare well in the journey.

With time and, of course, practice, you will start having a better grip on your emotions. That's when being self-disciplined would come easy to you. With better control over your emotion, focus more on responding to a situation instead of reacting to it- another golden rule to practice discipline and extend your willpower.

Respond with Intention or React with Impulse

We tend to give in to instant gratification and oblige our temptations when we react to a situation.

For example, when your alarm beeps, you may feel tempted to sleep. Your reaction to the situation- turn off the alarm and go back to dreamland.

You come across an advert for spaghetti with meatballs and a brownie. Your reaction to the situation- place an order and ruin your diet.

Every time you react, you potentially ruin the routine you have built over the past few days to hone your discipline.

What you truly need to do in its place is to respond to the situation.

Responding to a situation means you think it over when your emotions have calmed down, think things through, and then put your best foot forward. You may sometimes take the same course of action that you would have taken as a reaction, but when you respond, it means you have assessed every possible route and then used those observations to make a choice.

Mostly, reactions make us lose golden opportunities; they also sabotage our willpower. The willpower you have built up to a certain level gets shattered, and your efforts bear naught. To ensure this does not happen to you, train yourself to respond to situations and emotions.

- You already know how to stay strong when an intense emotion is doing the rounds in your body.
- Once you have calmed it down a notch, think of how to best behave in the situation.
- It is likely your urge to order a juicy burger or splurge on yourself would have decreased in intensity by now.
- Go back to your goal, focus on the bigger picture, and take out your compelling whys.
- Revisit the reasons why you began this journey to ensure that your willpower starts powering up.
- Now think of the best way forward. The chances are high that you will refuse the temptation and stay strong.

Every time you work on this routine, write down the decision you took. Sometimes, you may falter, and as I said before, that is okay. Learn from the experience, find out the key takeaways, and apply them to the new situation.

While responding to situations, pay special attention to the habits that delay your willpower.

Delay Habits that Drain Your Willpower

Certain habits are well-known willpower killers. Those are the ones you need to delay as much as possible. As you delay them, slowly get rid of them for good. We have already discussed how to pinpoint negative habits.

Out of those, some slowly deplete your willpower. For instance, not sleeping on time once may not affect your fitness plan too much, but when you do that regularly, even if you push back your sleep time by 10 minutes daily, you gradually lower your energy levels.

- Closely observe the habits you engage in and how they make you feel about your goal.
- When you observe one that affects your habit change schedule even the slightest bit, start to delay it.
- The best way to delay a habit that eats away at your willpower is to distract yourself from it. Sometimes, only excusing yourself from the situation does the trick. Use the hack to your advantage.
- Track how successfully you can delay those habits each time; that way, you will feel motivated to perform better the next time.

Delaying unhealthy habits becomes even easier when you modify your environment to support the habit change process.

Change the Environment

The environment you are in monumentally affects your decisions and actions. A study proved that when fizzy drinks in the refrigerators near the cash counter were replaced with bottled water, people switched to the former and made healthier choices. Sodas and carbonated beverages were still in the fridges at the back of the cafeteria, but bottled water was easily accessible to them, making the choice that much easier.

A simple modification in the environment made people opt for healthier choices. The crux of the matter is that changing the environment can help you stop allowing unconstructive habits to get the better of you.

- Pay attention to how your environment affects your behaviors.
- Look for elements that trigger certain habits, delay some behaviors, and encourage you to stick to some activities for long. Perhaps your room has dim lighting that makes you tired, prompting you to ditch your workout session. Maybe there is a TV in your workplace, encouraging you to switch it on instead of working.
- After identifying those factors, get rid of them as much as possible.
- Change the room's lighting, use an elliptical or treadmill to exercise while you work, ditch your phone when it is time for you to work. These little changes yield great results in the long run.
- In addition, make your environment as organized and de-cluttered as possible. Mess triggers laziness, keeping you from doing what's important. Imagine entering a cluttered room full of piles of clothes, socks, accessories, and maybe some trash in the corner. You couldn't possibly work in that room. Even if you had plans of reading a book peacefully, you would rather go someplace else. That is what clutters does to us: it derails and frustrates us.

  In such times, giving into instant gratification feels easy too. That is why you need to de-clutter your house, workplace, and whatever environment you work in or

where you practice certain activities. Get rid of the extras in the place; throw out the broken and used stuff and remove everything that doesn't bring you joy.
- Once you have de-cluttered your environment, organize everything neatly, ensuring a specific place for everything you decide to keep.
- Every few days, scan the space for anything unnecessary and remove it, so you keep it tidy and clutter-free.
- Ensure that you take special note of anything that contributes to your bad habits and addictions, so you can eliminate the triggers on time before they devour your willpower.

As your environment becomes more organized and peaceful with time, you become more in control of your emotions and temptations.

Just Do It

After creating a scheduling, you need to follow it. Unfortunately, doing this is often very difficult for most people, especially those prone to procrastination.

Getting started with a plan is difficult. Moreover, when you don't commence taking action on the plan, your temptations are likely to pull you into a rut. Want to change that for good? Here are some tips to help you do so:

- Firstly, get started with the first task on your list right away. Need to look up some fitness centers to start working out? Get on it. Have to send an email to a potential investor? Send right away. Kick start the journey with the smallest possible task you can carry out

right away, so you can at least begin implementing the plan. That little task gives you some motivation to build momentum, and slowly you start following through with it.
- Secondly, you could sometimes pick the most difficult task and work on it first. Also known as the 'eat an ugly frog' strategy, this technique works because it makes you take the hard step first. Once you have the most cumbersome task done, you know nothing is impossible for you: you can do anything!
- Moreover, visualize yourself reaching the finish line every time you need to work on a task. Close your eyes and see yourself becoming victorious. This practice charges you up, giving you the necessary push to move further towards your goals.
- Every time you work on a task, observe your performance and assess it in detail. Point out the flaws, areas where you erred, and whether or not you could fix the issue. Use this as a guideline to do better the next time.

During the process, you may feel the inclination to push yourself too much or overdo things. When you notice that, you need to go easy on yourself.

Don't Push Yourself Too Much

When you are trying to achieve a goal, you may become too hard on yourself, trying to do as much as possible at once or going too far with a certain practice. For instance, you may push yourself to work out for 60 minutes the first time you do it after a decade. You may pull that off that time around only to have a sore body the next day that doesn't even let you get up.

In that process, you only hurt your willpower. When you cannot work on your action plan the next day, you aren't getting any meaningful results. Is there any way to stop this issue? Yes, there is: you go easy on yourself.

- Make sure to always start with one habit at a time. I have said it again but let me emphasize it to ensure you practice it.
- Space out your tasks by adding breaks between them. Breaks give you the much-needed cushion you need to relax and energize yourself to ensure you don't go crazy.
- Don't fret about getting 100% results all the time. It is okay if you were aiming for a 30-minute workout but could only do it for 20 minutes. Start being comfortable with settling for good enough. You can do that by telling yourself that it is okay to settle for good enough results and improve your performance the next time around.
- When you have a bad day, stop trying to get results. Take a day off and get back to your plan with a fresh mind and a well-rested body.

You may not be able to do all this right now, but once you carry out these tasks, you will realize how calming and empowering they are.

Get Sufficient Sleep

Notice your mood and behavior if you go sleep-deprived for just a day. You will feel cranky, short-tempered, and would most likely want to go back to bed. Now imagine how this feeling will only increase if you continue to cut back on your sleep intake. *Research* also shows that sleep impacts your willpower. The less you sleep, the higher your chances of giving in to your temptations and struggle to practice self-control.

Why put yourself through this misery when you can easily get your job done by sleeping well at night. Ensure to get around 7 to 9 hours of sleep on average every night. This is the recommended sleep intake for adults, and if you are sleeping fewer hours than that, you are only keeping yourself from feeling healthy, happy, and disciplined.

- Set a fixed bedtime and hit the bed about half an hour before that, if not more.
- In that half an hour, relax and carry out some deep breathing exercises to unwind. The calmer you feel, the easier it is to initiate sleep.
- Try doing some relaxing activity an hour or two before you hit the bed. For example, take a warm shower if possible, read a soothing book, or listen to some soulful music. Of course, these aren't the only options at your disposal. You can do whatever calms you down and relaxes you before you hit the bed.
- Also, wake up at a fixed time every day; that way, you will train yourself to sleep and rise at a set time, which will become part of your routine. Make sure you get 7 hours of sleep in between those times.

It will take you a couple of weeks to adjust to this routine, but soon enough, you will get there. While doing so, ensure to feed yourself well.

Eat Well

Along with pushing yourself too much, not eating well also depletes your willpower. What you feed yourself affects your energy levels. You may feel energized after a good sugar rush from having a couple of sodas, but that doesn't last long. Also, the processed sugar and chemicals in the drink only weaken your body in the long run.

To perform well, stay put when distractions come your way and always think clearly, you need a strong body. Here's how you can attain that:

- Have a healthy breakfast in the morning. Fill it up with proteins, healthy carbohydrates, good fats, fiber, and vitamin sources such as whole wheat grains, oatmeal, bran bread, eggs, avocadoes, beans, lean meat cuts, and a piece or two of fruit.
- Ensure to have your breakfast about 30 to 60 minutes after waking up, don't wait any longer than that, or you will starve yourself.
- Slowly get rid of processed, packaged, frozen, and junk foods in your diet as it is usually rich in saturated trans-fats, genetically modified organisms, processed chemicals, and harmful ingredients.
- Add more fresh fruits, vegetables such as leafy greens, lean meat cuts, whole wheat grains, organic dairy products, soy goods, nuts, and lots of water to your diet.
- Space out your meals during the day to ensure that you keep supplying yourself with a constant stream of energy throughout the day, especially when you are working or need to engage in high-priority tasks pertinent to your goal.

While eating well, look after your fitness too because it directly affects your self-discipline as well.

Get Moving, Get Active

Just as your diet and sleep affect your health and ability to practice self-control, physical fitness does so.

In a study[1], participants had to exercise for two months. During the study, researchers tested them on a range of self-control activities that required them to resist temptations and persevere through tough tasks. The results were phenomenal!

Researchers observed that the participants had improved their ability to overcome temptations, persevere in tough times, procrastinated less, had better emotional control, and successfully reduced their caffeine and alcohol intake. They also smoked less, consumed less junk food, saved more money, binge-watched fewer television shows, began eating healthier foods, studied better, and improved the overall productivity of the different areas of their lives.

Why am I telling you this? To encourage you to start exercising more and often. Getting up and moving around more may seem challenging at the moment, but in reality, it is quite easy.

Here's what you need to do:

- Walk more during the day. Instead of staying on the couch, directing people to do things for you, like getting a glass of water or switching on the AC, get up and do the tasks yourself.

---

[1] https://www.willpowered.co/learn/effects-of-exercise-on-willpower

- Ditch the elevator whenever possible; use the stairs instead.
- Instead of getting groceries delivered to your place, walk to the store if it is just around the corner.
- Add in some form of physical activity in your life. You could cycle, play a sport you like such as badminton or basketball, go for a swim, or dance vigorously.
- Exercise for about 10 minutes daily. You could do some jumping jacks, crunches, push-ups, mountain climbers, or just some stretches followed by a walk or jog. Do whatever feels convenient at the start, but at least do it. Increase the duration of your exercise routine slowly to take it up to 30 to 40 minutes.

It is only a matter of time before you observe a massive improvement in your stamina and strength. You will find it easier to focus on one task, complete projects on time, and think clearly every time you have to choose between your temptation and task. To keep the ball rolling, never forget to reward yourself for your hard work throughout the process.

Reward Yourself

Think of the time your boss rewarded you for all your hard work and excellent performance at work. That reward, even if it was just a certificate of acknowledgment, felt good, right? That's how rewards work: they make you feel great about yourself; they fuel your intrinsic motivation.

Apply this rule to your self-discipline journey too. Set milestones for yourself to achieve, and every time you climb up a level, reward yourself with something you enjoy. Sometimes, it could be a pat on the back, a few words of encouragement, a trip to the shopping mall, treating yourself to ice cream, buying yourself a new phone, going on a dinner date with your partner, or simply sleeping in over the weekend.

To see the worth of those rewards, record your feelings in your journal shortly after treating yourself to one reward. Go through these accounts once weekly to realize how worthwhile rewards are. This little tip ensures you reward yourself well on every milestone accomplished and keep moving forwards to your goal.

While you are at it, train yourself not to engage in self-sabotage because it is a potential danger that can ruin your self-discipline journey. Let us talk about it in the next part of the book.

PART 6

DEFEATING SELF-SABOTAGE

'Self-sabotage is when we say we want something, and then go about making sure it doesn't happen.'

—Alyce Cornyn- Selby

If you have worked on achieving the same goal repeatedly and always found yourself lost midway through, perhaps you are doing things that are sabotaging your progress. Self-sabotage often happens most discreetly. You don't consciously see it happen, but you are doing all the right things to bring it about in your life in one way or another.

Let us discuss how you potentially ruin your chances of empowering your self-control with self-sabotaging behaviors and ways to overcome them.

Understanding Self-Sabotage

Self-sabotage is when your conscious mind does not come to terms with your subconscious mind. Your conscious side is the one that reminds you to save money, exercise, sleep on time, eat healthily, and the likes, whereas the subconscious side convinces you to stress-eat, go on shopping binges online, and sleep in till late in the afternoon. The two are quite at odds with each other when it comes to building self-control.

When this happens, you engage in thoughts, behaviors, and practices that obstruct you from achieving what you desire the most in life. The subconscious voice at the back of your mind is your internal sentiment, constantly gnawing at you, telling you how you cannot achieve something.

As hurtful as it seems, your subconscious is trying to keep you from going through failures and dealing with your deep-seated fears. How is that so?

How Self-Sabotage is a Coping Mechanism Meant to Save Us

Back in the days of the early man, life was quite different. The challenges early men faced were quite extraordinary. Escaping avalanches, fighting saber-tooth tigers, and fleeing from flocks of holy mammoths was the norm of that time. The development of the human brain happened according to the challenges too.

The most primitive region of the human brain triggers your fight, flight, or freeze response, aka the stress response, the instant it fears that you are facing some danger. Physiological changes occur in your body, such as extensive blood flow to the limbs, rapid heartbeat, tightening of muscles, etc., so you can cope with the harmful situation.

As humans and the situation evolved, so did the human brain. That said, the primitive human brain is still intact and working. It still operates on the same fear of survival and fires up when it senses even an ounce of a danger approaching you.

When we diet, work out or set any other goal that is difficult for us to pursue or is something we haven't tried in a long time, our primitive brain becomes active. It starts to become cautious and scared for us. It fears something wrong may happen, and so it begins creating the 'what if' scenarios in our heads. If you are starting on the self-control journey, you are likely to give in to these apprehensions easily.

It is also important to understand that we are the ones who strengthen this negative inner voice and our tendency to give in to the fears brewed by our primitive minds. How? By engaging in various self-sabotaging practices.

The result of these practices is always unfavorable for you.

How Self-Sabotage Ruins You

You wouldn't probably go after your dreams when you doubt your potential.

You are quite likely to forego your goals when you constantly give in to your challenges.

You find it difficult to stay steadfast on the right path when all you do is shatter your willpower.

You cannot stay focused and optimistic when you constantly demoralize yourself by engaging in negative self-talk.

You cannot take charge of your life when you constantly blame others for the mishaps you go through.

You find it difficult to achieve your goals when you hang out with toxic people.

You falter time and again when you have a whining attitude in life.

The list can go on and on. The case I am trying to make is: you cannot have different wins to your credit if you continue doing things that sabotage your growth and success.

That's why you need to be your biggest ally, and for that, you must let go of self-sabotage.

If you often worry about how you missed out on many golden opportunities in life but don't know exactly why that happened, understand that self-sabotage was a key player in the equation.

Different Self-Sabotaging Behaviors You Should Know

Let us take a look at the different self-sabotaging behaviors and practices that demand your attention.

Talking Negatively to Yourself

We tend to doubt our capabilities, which affects our willpower when we talk negatively to ourselves. Years of downplaying our strengths, being overly critical of our abilities, and not acknowledging our efforts give rise to our inner critic, a mean, inner voice that has nothing kind to offer us.

Every time the going gets tougher, the inner critic fires up, ready to remind you of your shortcomings. You don't want to get pulled back by your inner voice this time around, right? You have come quite far, and you wouldn't want to go back to the old situation. To only keep going upwards and onwards, here's how you can improve on that inner critic and train yourself to develop positive self-talk.

- Pay attention to how you talk to yourself.
- Every time you notice a hint of negativity in your thoughts and suggestions, hold onto that suggestion and write it down.
- Omit negative words from it and reframe it with more positive words. For instance, if you had thought, 'I cannot exercise today,' or 'Eating healthy is impossible,' change it to, 'I am going to exercise,' and 'Eating healthy is fun and doable.'
- Similarly, for suggestions such as, 'I am a loser,' 'I can never discipline myself,' and 'I am destined for failure,' replace them with, 'I am a winner,' 'I am disciplined,' and 'success is my destiny.'
- Chant the reframed suggestion a few times until it settles in your mind.

Don't treat this practice as a one-off thing. Engage in it several times during the day to slowly shape up the habit of positively talking to yourself at all times.

Not Taking Accountability for Your Actions

We have all been down that rabbit hole when we blamed others for our problems. However, some of us are guilty of adopting this demeanor for good. No matter what goes wrong in our lives, we always find someone else to blame for it.

This behavior is self-sabotaging because it keeps you from taking accountability for your actions. Not feeling responsible for your actions and decisions keeps you from bettering the situation yourself.

To get out of that vicious cycle, start taking accountability for your decisions:

- Every time something goes wrong, don't look for someone else to blame.
- Accept that a mishap happened and own it.
- You could say something such as, 'I missed a day of workout because I was lazy.' The instant you say it out loud, you own your decision instead of blaming it on your partner.
- At the end of each day, analyze the consequences of your actions and brainstorm ideas to improve them.

Spending Time with the Wrong Sort of People

Jim Rohn once said,

> *'You are the average of the five people you spend the most time with.'*

What does it mean?

Simply put, it means you are the company you keep. When you spend most of your time with people prone to addictions and lacking self-control in their life, their insecurities, fears, and behaviors are bound to rub off on you. As a result, you start behaving the same way, and before you realize it, you quit your goals.

Surely, you don't want that to be your fate. In that case, stop spending time with the toxic influences in your life. How can you identify them? They could be the following kinds of people:

- Those who ridicule you
- Those who remind you of your failures, keeping you from believing in yourself
- Those who don't take charge of their life
- Those who lack self-control and self-discipline
- Those who focus on the negatives of a situation only
- Those consumed by their fears and insecurities
- Those who keep you from dreaming big

Start slowly distancing yourself from such influences and surround yourself with those who uplift your spirits, believe in you, follow their dreams, are self-disciplined, and empower you.

Complaining about Your Problems All the Time

Your life is a manifestation of what you practice. You complain, your life becomes laden with problems. On the other hand, if you build the courage to focus on the positives, you practice gratitude and contentment, leading to better outcomes.

When it comes to self-control, it is crucial to be grateful. Let me tell you why. While trying to practice self-control, there may come a time when you falter and fail to follow the schedule. In case of such mishaps, it is very easy to lose focus and give in to instant gratification, which prompts you to surrender to your temptations and lose your control.

On the other hand, if you choose to focus on your blessings in life, you stay positive. You know it is okay to have setbacks, so you don't bash yourself when that happens. Instead, you use gratitude to stay steadfast on your journey. You get back up, refuel your motivation and resume the journey.

Gratitude keeps you grounded, humble, positive, and focused. Here's how you can practice it:

- Start your day on a note of gratitude by thinking of the one blessing you feel the most grateful for that day.
- Take short two-minute gratitude breaks every few hours. Think of any two to three things you wish to acknowledge and go through their importance in your life.
- Every time you encounter a challenge, instead of complaining about how it ruins your life, think of how it improves your life. For example, even if you haven't been able to eat healthy for a while, you can do it now by observing your eating patterns better.
- In challenging times, shift your focus towards your blessings and use that positivity to power through the problems.

You may take this lightly right now, but you'll honestly be amazed at how much being grateful benefits you in the long run.

Not Getting to the Root of the Issue

You can complain all you want about how unfair your life is, but if you aren't getting to the bottom of problems, you aren't getting anywhere. Self-sabotage is also when you keep making the same mistakes repeatedly, thereby never getting the desired results.

A major reason why this happens is that you don't get to the bottom of the problem.

If you are constantly losing your self-control, trying different diets only to gain more weight, and never get any luck with any of your goals, perhaps you aren't tackling the actual issue.

- Keeping in view your self-control agenda and action plan, think of where you are going wrong.
- Ask yourself powerful questions such as: Why am I not getting the desired results? What do I need to improve? Where do I lack? What is the precise problem?
- As you start to get some answers, further probe into them. For instance, if you are asking yourself why you keep skipping your workout, perhaps the answer you get is: it is too difficult. From there, you can then ask yourself, how can I make it easier? Maybe the answer is to go slow or to choose another routine. Similarly, probe into the answers you get concerning a problem until you get to the bottom of it.
- Once you have the root cause in front of you, find out ways to fix it. You know what the lack of self-control boils down to, so start taking intentional action to resolve it.

You have come forward a long way, and there is no looking back now because you will go even further. Make sure to get rid of self-sabotage slowly but for good. As you work on it, also work on the six important habits of self-control. The next part focuses on that specifically.

PART 7

THE 6 HABITS OF SELF-CONTROL

"To handle yourself, use your head; to handle others, use your heart."

—Donald Laird

Your head—basically what you know and believe—your mind and heart, are your biggest assets. If you use them right, you become unstoppable. To do that successfully, you need to master the art of building self-control.

So far, you have been doing very well and, this course will accelerate your learning even more once you learn the six phenomenal habits of self-control.

Right now, let's dive in and optimize these habits.

1. Focus on One Habit (and Behavior) at a Time

We discussed this strategy in an earlier section of the book. Why am I sharing it again? That's because when we try to discipline ourselves, we often get carried away by the process. While trying to do too much, or become even better than before, we start to fill up our plate with so many tasks, activities, or various 'good' ideas. That's when you are likely to force yourself to work on multiple habits at the same time.

You may try to quit smoking, exercise daily, work 10 hours a day, increase your clientele, and beat procrastination all at the same time. You may manage to handle this for a couple of days, but your willpower will collapse soon because you are not in the habit of exerting too much pressure on yourself. You will end up frustrated, burned-out, and drift back to the old, familiar habits that exist inside your comfort zone.

That is why you must always start with one habit.

- Pick the area of your life you want to improve first.
- In that area, select any one improvement you wish to

achieve. For example, if your health matters to you and currently diagnosed with diabetes type II but are determined to control it, you could work on it.

- Create a meaningful goal based on the improvement you aspire to make. In this case, it could be, 'I want to control my diabetes and control my blood sugar level.'
- Next, identify all the unhealthy habits you currently have pertinent to that improvement you want. If your blood sugar level is exceedingly high, is it because you eat calorie-rich foods, because you don't walk, or because you are prone to chronic stress? There could be other reasons too.
- Make a list of the habits you need to work on, so once you complete working on a habit, you work on the next one in line.
- Once you have identified the key areas that demand your attention, pick one habit you wish to break and replace it with a healthier one.
- Next, create a habit change plan based on it, as taught earlier, and get to work.
- If you want to build a certain habit individually, not necessarily in place of an existing habit, identify the area, create a goal on it, make a plan of action, and get started with it. For instance, if you want to read more books, figure out the kinds of books you wish to read, why you want to do so, have your compelling reasons ready, create milestones, have your action plan in place, and start working on it right away.

After completing a specific goal, revisit your list of habits, and work your way up to another.

2. Create Incremental Goals

Incremental is an adjective that refers to an increase in something. Add this adjective to your goals to turn them into 'incremental goals.' What are they? Well, they are extremely powerful and lend quite a helping hand to you when you embark on the journey to empower your self-control.

I have mentioned a couple of times earlier in the book how your willpower starts to drop unbearably low when you take on a goal as a whole. For example, if someone asks you to read a 600-page book, you will likely go bonkers only thinking of it, let alone opening the first page.

Imagine your brain going through the same problem when you make a public announcement to become sugar-free in two weeks, lose 30 pounds, or quit smoking. These goals may sound immensely big and empowering at first, but in the long run, such big claims mostly make you go through a downward spiral of troubles.

Announcing something big sounds good to your ears and mind. When you challenge yourself, you feel excited. A surge of adrenaline, the hormone responsible for both stress and excitement, occurs in your body. This adrenaline rush makes you feel elated. However, the rush soon dies down. When it does, you realize how overwhelming the **BIG GOAL** is, and that's when the reality starts to sink in: it is **difficult!**

Usually, in such circumstances, most of us give up. While using different excuses such as your goal being too big, wanting different things in life, or not setting the correct and meaningful goal, you quit it.

In actuality, the problem does not lie in any of these areas. It stems from not making that goal realistic enough. This is where incremental goals come in handy. They make your huge, overpowering goal more manageable and doable. Instead of taking up something tremendous as a whole, you chop it down to make it more breathable.

If someone told you to read two pages of a book every day, naturally, that feels easier to manage. You know it will take you about 15 minutes maximum, and within only 15 minutes, you will have completed the task. On the contrary, when someone asks you to read a 500-page book, it feels pressurizing even if you have about a month to finish the book.

That is why I always focus on setting incremental goals; I advise you to do the same. Here's how you can do that.

- Take your big goal and chop it into a medium-term milestone. For example, if you want to lose 30 pounds in a year, your medium-term goal can be to lose 15 pounds in six months.
- Take that medium-term goal and chop it down into a short-term goal, say lose 7.5 pounds in three months.
- Focus on this short-term goal and further butcher it into weekly milestones to ensure that you have a target to achieve every week. If you wish to lose 7.5 pounds in three months, it means you have about 12 weeks. You could easily lose around 0.5 pounds every week.
- Now focus on what you need to do to achieve that goal. If you decide to lose weight with the help of aerobics, pick a starting point. For instance, you could start with doing aerobics for 10 minutes a day. Then, you need to slowly increase the duration every week to turn it into an incremental goal. Here's how your incremental goals should look like:

- Work out for 10 minutes 6 days a week in week
- Work out for 15 minutes 6 days a week in week
- Work out for 20 minutes 6 days a week in week
- Work out for 20 minutes 6 days a week in week
- Work out for 25 minutes 6 days a week in week
- Work out for 25 minutes 6 days a week in week
- Work out for 30 minutes 6 days a week in week
- Work out for 30 minutes 6 days a week in week

- Use this process to keep building on the goal until you start working out for the desired amount of time every day.

As you follow through with your incremental goals, you will start noticing positive results and shall move closer to your goal. Also, this process does not exhaust you because you build up to the desired success instead of pushing yourself too hard and knocking yourself out in the process.

3. Set Clear Cravings Boundaries

Clarity is one of the golden keys to success in any area of your life. The clearer you are on what you want, the easier it becomes to achieve it. How do I say that with surety? Because that's how I have transformed my life for the better in every aspect of life.

When it comes to building self-control, you need to be clear on everything, especially when it comes to setting up boundaries for your cravings. Decide on what you wish to control, why you need to do so, how much of it you should control, and how to go about it.

The clearer your boundaries are, the better you follow them, and the faster you move towards your end goal. Clear boundaries refer to knowing the limits you need to follow and when to observe them.

- Focusing on the habit you wish to change, think of the distractions you are likely to experience.
- If you have already identified them as taught earlier, go through them.
- Analyze every distraction, every temptation in-depth, and think of the boundary you need to have in place. For instance, if you know you will feel tempted to eat a hamburger after two days of not eating it, maybe the boundary could be to eat half a burger on the third day and treat yourself to a full burger when you stick to the diet for a week.

  If you decide not to tend to unexpected visitors during your work hours in your home office, think of how to communicate that boundary to them. Perhaps you could send off such visitors, not attend their calls, or refuse them politely if they show up.
- Once you decide which boundaries to set, write them down and go through them at least twice daily: once in the daytime and once before going to bed. Checking them when the day starts reminds you of what you ought to do in the day and going through them before dozing off alerts your subconscious to focus on the boundaries better.
- Make sure to revisit your boundaries and check your performance on them every few days. For instance, if you have been refusing to meet friends during your work hours, gauge your sentiments. Has it been easy for you to say no? When has it been difficult? How can you make

the transition even smoother? Focus on the root cause, and you'll easily discover the answers.

You will stand astonished at how quickly you skyrocket your success once you start setting clear boundaries and communicating them to yourself and others with more clarity.

4. Make a Reward System

A system of rewards is crucial to progress in life. I discussed rewarding yourself briefly earlier. Now I want to dig deeper into the aspect.

Rewarding yourself is a crucial part of success because it gives you that dose of excitement. It gives you the adrenaline rush and dopamine you need to feel good about yourself.

You already know what adrenaline does to you. Now, let's talk about dopamine a little. Dopamine is the 'reward chemical.' Both it and adrenaline and many other chemicals are hormones your body produces naturally when triggered by certain outside agents. Dopamine makes you feel good about yourself; it improves your happiness, confidence, and enthusiasm levels. There are four main ways to enjoy a good surge of dopamine:

- Completing a task
- Celebrating little victories
- Engaging in self-care activities
- Eating food

All these four aspects pertain to self-control. When you complete a milestone, your dopamine levels improve. When you celebrate those wins and reward yourself, your dopamine levels rise again.

One common way to rejoice over a victory is to celebrate

over a plate of food, which once again spikes your dopamine levels. Moreover, while building your self-control, you are likely to engage in self-care activities that do wonders for your dopamine concentration.

When you engage in these activities, you like yourself better, feel self-motivated and find it easier to stick to your goals and fulfill them.

Having established how rewarding yourself keeps you invigorated, let us focus on creating a reward system.

First, let me clarify why you need to have a rewards system and not just one reward that you treat yourself with once in a blue moon.

Having a rewards system means you set a range of different rewards for different milestones and engage in them every time you achieve a certain milestone. Instead of using the same reward every time, you entice yourself with something fresh and uplifting as you work towards something you truly want to do or achieve. This keeps your interest alive in the journey.

Sadly, sometimes we use a certain reward to the extent that it stops feeling like a reward. For example, because you have a pizza takeout every time you complete a buyer's order that now, it feels routine to you. It no longer excites you, and when it doesn't please you, you stop taking it seriously. That's when you slowly or sometimes even very quickly start losing interest in your goal as well.

Carrying on with this, another mistake many of us make when setting rewards is to use the same prize for every kind of victory. For example, you may go shopping for clothes whether you have lost 5 pounds or 7 pounds or even 20. This also reduces your interest in the goal because it makes you feel as if your efforts aren't appreciated enough.

The best way to handle these issues is to build a foolproof reward system.

- For every habit change plan, you have already identified the milestones.
- Assess the nature of the milestones and how you feel about each target. For instance, working out for 10 minutes a day may not be a huge task. However, since you haven't exercised in half a decade, it could be monumental for you.
- Once you have assessed what a milestone means to you, give it a certain ranking: important, very important, most important, or something along these lines.
- Next, think of some healthy rewards you could treat yourself to after completing the milestone. The rewards could even be something unhealthy in a controlled amount. For instance, treating yourself to a slice of chocolate cake after two months of healthy dieting and portion control is fine as long as you don't go overboard with it and treat yourself to the entire cake.
- Put down all the rewards in your journal, and describe how valuable they are for you, each at a time.
- Complement every milestone with a corresponding reward based on its importance for you. If going on a week-long vacation is the most valuable reward, enjoy it when you have been staying true to your fitness-based action plan for two months.
- Peg every milestone to a reward and put it down on your calendar—Google Calendar[2] is a great app that can

---

[2] https://calendar.google.com/calendar/u/0/r

simplify your life. Use it for this purpose and to create all your other routine schedules.
- Stick to the reward system and keep a close eye on it. Every time you are close to achieving a target, spend some moments reflecting on what that accomplishment can do for you, and you'll feel even more energized to achieve that feat.

As you implement the fixed reward system, analyze it routinely to check whether it works for you. If a certain reward lacks luster or isn't effective enough to keep you hooked to your target, replace it with something more rewarding.

5. Beware of Triggers and Emotional Switches

Clarity is essential. It matters when it comes to setting your goals and boundaries, and also when it comes to knowing your emotional switches and triggers.

We are bound to experience different emotions in different life situations. Even when we have complete command of them, we experience them, which is good and proper. Our emotions give us insight into how we feel, how different factors affect us, and how our reaction or response shapes our life. As you start to become emotionally aware, aim to understand your emotions very well, including their influence on your behaviors and life.

- After deciding to work on a particular habit, once again, examine how you engage in it, what triggers that habit, and why you stick to it.
- Take each of these three parts of the habit loop and think of the emotions at play in the loop. For instance, if you smoke when your friend visits you, what emotions do

you experience then? Do you smoke with him to rejoice, or is it because you want to vent out your frustrations via a couple of smokes with a friend?
- It is okay to pinpoint as many emotions affecting a respective habit as possible. Write them down.
- Also, identify all the possible emotions at play for each of the three: trigger, routine, and reward. An easy way to do that is to ask yourself questions such as: Do I feel relieved when I do this? Or does it help me mitigate stress? Or does it provide me with pleasure?
- Now focus on looking for these possible emotions when you are about to engage in a specific behavior.
- When exactly do you feel stressed before having a smoke? Do you have a headache before that? Or do you feel overburdened, and that looming feeling leads to stress and then smoking?
- Start looking for these symptoms, and when you identify them, start working on managing those emotional cues and triggers.
- Look for ways to calm yourself down. I'll share some valuable exercises in the following chapter to help you out.
- As already discussed, you can also distract yourself with different activities. Emotions that trigger temptations aren't real. Once you distract yourself, you lose focus on them. That's when you need to remind yourself of what you ought to do in actuality to divert your attention towards it.
- Moreover, name the emotion you can feel in that moment and verbally acknowledge that you are experiencing it. You can even write that down. For example, if you are

sad and feel like having a drink or two, say, 'I feel sad and want to drink.' Once you have verbally acknowledged that emotional trigger and temptation, take a deep breath and ask yourself if that's what you genuinely want.

For example, you could say, 'Am I just tempted to do it, or do I really want it?' Trust that you will get a very clear answer. Now it is on you not to ignore the genuine answer, and instead, oblige it by **not giving into the trigger**.

Like with everything else, keeping track of your emotional cues is crucial as well, so you get a deeper comprehension of which emotions you are getting a better hang on and which ones need more supervision.

6. Focus on the Bigger Picture to get Long-Term Growth and Sustainable Habits

You didn't get to where you are in life within the blink of an eye, right? For anything meaningful to stay in your life, you have to focus on building long-term, sustainable habits. Likewise, you cannot empower your self-control, build powerful habits and reclaim your life with the snap of your fingers.

When you try to become healthier, build a long-term commitment to it. If you want to become physically fit, don't just think of losing the extra 10 pounds, but focus on building muscle strength. Don't stop working out or eating healthier once you reach your desired weight, but inculcate that habit for the long run, ensuring it stays with you and ensures you stay in the best possible physical, mental, and emotional state.

Here are some key ideas to focusing on the bigger picture to create long-term growth.

Always keep your core values in sight. Go through them at least a couple of times every week and ask yourself if you genuinely follow them. If you get 'no' as an answer in any one area, think of what you may not be doing right and how you can fix the issue.

Keep building on your compelling reasons every week. You know how to dig them out, right? Carry out that practice regularly to ensure you identify more reasons why you wish to achieve a goal and empower your self-control. We are constantly changing: the situations, experiences, and different nuances we go through in life influence us. That means our compelling reasons should change too, sometimes not entirely, but in intensity or form with some modifications.

Perhaps you may now feel strongly about making moments in your life count and living healthier now that you have seen a friend lose her loved one. Maybe now that you sense body pains, you realize how important it is to give up on fast food and eat healthier. Our compelling reasons are open to change. Accept this reality, then commit to revisiting and building on them over time to identify more reasons why you need unwavering commitment to build or break a respective habit.

Make visualization a constant part of your life. Everyday, think of making it to the finish line. Play that video in your head repeatedly, and when you see yourself becoming triumphant in the end, focus on the particular emotion you experience in that time. Name it.

Is it confidence, happiness, excitement, trust, joy, exactly what? Now, you need to anchor the emotion to a certain gesture, such as snapping your fingers, pressing two fingers, tapping your arm, or anything else. This is a neuro-linguistic programming (NLP) technique that helps rewire the way you think and feel.

You anchor that emotion with the respective gesture, such that every time you practice the gesture, you experience the particular emotion. This technique allows you to feel happy, strong, confident, etc., all within a couple of moments.

Ensure that you practice the chosen gesture a couple of times when thinking of the emotion to anchor the two successfully. Now try the gesture and sense if you can feel the emotion. If you don't feel it right away, go through the steps again. Every time you feel like you are losing your grip over your emotions, envision yourself making it to the finish line and try the anchoring technique; you'll regain your strength and get back on track.

These six habits of self-control are what you need to get everything in order. You can do it all if you work on all of these, but please remember to do it one by one. To do that right, supplement the process by managing your energy, exercising, and relaxing more often.

"People may flatter themselves just as much by thinking that their faults are always present to other people's minds, as if they believe that the world is always contemplating their individual charms and virtues."

—Elizabeth Gaskel

PART 8

MANAGING ENERGY, EXERCISE, AND RELAXATION

*'Your mind will answer most questions
if you learn to relax and wait for the answer.'*

—William S. Burroughs

I have mentioned that your mind gives you the right answers when you ask it the right questions framed positively. However, we often cannot ask ourselves constructive questions because we are too rushed, stressed, or exhausted.

For example, there may have been times when you wanted to ask yourself how important your goals are to you or how to develop self-control, but because you felt drained, you rushed to surrender to the temptation that came your way. Perhaps you did not want to give in to the urge to have a soda but did it anyway because you were overwhelmed with stress.

Such issues happen, and it's okay.

However, we are in it to improve, right?

You want to empower your self-control, right?

You want to become a stronger, more confident, and emotionally stable individual who lives life his/her way, right?

In that case, you have to learn to manage your energy and relax so that every time you feel swamped by an individual temptation or sense your self-control wavering, you can manage it easily.

Here are some helpful exercises for you.

The Square Breathing Technique

Deep breathing is a powerful means of calming yourself down and having a better grip on frenzied thoughts and intense emotions. When you feel stressed, your stress response activates, and one of the physiological changes you experience in that time is your breath becoming rapid and shallow.

Therefore, when you generally take shallow and rapid breaths, you unconsciously send the stress signal to your brain. You don't want the stress hormones, primarily cortisol and adrenaline, to stay in your body for far too long. In that case, it is important to improve your breathing pattern. That is where deep breathing comes in handy.

Deep, long and calm breaths send a calming signal to your brain. When the brain senses that everything is okay, it switches on the parasympathetic response in your body, helping you manage your nerves and relax. We have already discussed a basic breathing technique.[3]

Here is another effective technique that can help you keep emotions in check to ensure that you put your best foot forward.

The Box Breathing Technique

Also called the square breathing technique, this is a very simple-to-practice technique that creates a paradigm shift in your stress levels within minutes. You need to breathe in equal parts, inhaling and exhaling through your nose and mouth, respectively, to create a box or square of sorts with your breath. Here's how you can do it.

- Sit calmly in a peaceful room or any other place.
- Rest your arms on your side, and gently close your eyes.
- Pace yourself for a couple of moments.
- Inhale to a count of 4 through your nose and observe your breath calmly.
- Hold that breath for a while, while your tummy inflates

---

[3] https://www.uofmhealth.org/health-library/uz2255

- to another count of 4.
- Keep watching your breath during this time.
- Now slowly exhale to the third count of 4, and make sure to exhale via your mouth.
- Hold your out-breath to the last round of 4.
- Practice these steps for about 2 to 5 minutes or about 10 to 15 times in total.
- You can also practice them until you sense your stress levels dropping down.

Practice this technique a couple of times every day. It is best to do it every time you have to execute a task from your plan of action, before every difficult task, and every time you sense stress stirring up inside your body. Stick to the practice, and you will get very comfortable with it in a week or two. At that point, it will start feeling natural to you, helping you reap great results.

Go Slow

We are often so rushed all the time that it almost seems as if we are meant to do more and be more, from being perfect at work to having the best relationships to having a passionate life with your partner to having a perfectly toned body to being great at co-curricular activities to building extra skills to having a life outside of work to what not. You have so many things that you need to do or feel that you ought to do that overburden you.

In that process, it is natural to compromise on certain things. That's when your temptations hit you and make it difficult for you to steadfast. Perhaps you are trying to excel at work and have been staying awake, burning the midnight oil for many days. You have also been working out from your office gym and eating perfectly healthy.

While you feel in control of yourself, your body is slowly zoning out. You need rest, but you don't let yourself have that break. You may start missing out on workouts, become short-tempered, or start gravitating towards calorie-rich foods in hopes of feeling comforted.

If you are prone to such problems, it shows you have been forcing yourself to do so much all the time. It is quite visible that your body and mind too cannot handle this much stress.

What's the best way to manage the situation?

Well, you train yourself to slow down. That's how you can best manage your emotions and energy, build and sustain your willpower, and slowly focus on things you want to do, not those that you feel pressured to engage in for this or that reason.

Slowing down is the art of not compelling yourself to do everything all the time and to live the perfect life as dictated by societal norms. It refers to doing things that spark joy for you, building habits that you really want, engaging in projects that add value to your life, and being with people who truly matter the most to you.

It is okay if you cannot be a millionaire, have six-packs, find the most compatible partner, and be an expert at music, linguistics, science, and so on. It is perfectly alright to focus on doing a few things at a time and keep your plate filled with just what you can handle. To achieve that, here's what you should start doing more:

- Take out the journal entry where you jotted down the most important aspects of your life.
- Pick any area you feel strongly about right now and think of how it feels overwhelming. What isn't right

about it? For example, if you have chosen to reflect on your work life, have you taken up projects that you don't feel connected to or are intrinsically motivated to pursue? Do you feel swamped with work? Are you involved in far too many activities relevant to work?
- Once you figure out the problematic areas, revert to your core values, and think about what truly matters to you.
- Write down those reflections.
- Now, think of the different improvements you can bring in your life following those realizations. Perhaps if you are a copywriter in a firm but have also started freelancing on the sideline, you need to choose between them to reduce your extra workload.
- While making different choices, ask yourself what really matters. Whether you want more money or mental peace? Whether your health matters or trying to prove yourself to others? Be comfortable with asking yourself such hard questions, and I assure you answers will come to you.
- Start paying heed to those answers, and slowly get rid of the extras in your life. This applies to the other aspects of your life too.
- Gradually, disengage from activities you don't enjoy. If you started playing tennis just to please your partner, let him/her know how the sport doesn't interest you. Being honest helps you save your willpower that you can use to work on other habits such as quitting smoking, going to bed on time, and the likes.
- Moreover, train yourself to do one task at a time. Liberate yourself from the undue pressure of doing everything at once and being perfect. Be comfortable with doing what you can and being happy with it.

As you start implementing these guidelines in your life, you will slowly see your energy and stamina levels rising. You will feel more energetic than before because you don't keep wasting your energy on doing meaningless things.

Go on a Digital Detox

As brilliant as it is, the internet and technology can be equally draining and sabotaging.

No, I am not saying the internet or digital technologies are bad. What I am saying is that too much of everything can be toxic. French fries are delicious, right? But what happens if you have them thrice a day for a month? Naturally, you lean towards obesity and fall at the risk of having high blood cholesterol levels.

Similarly, digital technologies are fantastic, but going overboard with them tends to exhaust you emotionally and psychologically. The blue rays emitted by these screens affect your circadian rhythm, which is your body's natural sleep-regulating clock. This is why you find it difficult to initiate sleep easily, especially after using the phone or computer for long hours before your bedtime.[4]

In addition, tech addiction is a known cause of stress and anxiety. A study shows that those who are addicted to digital technologies rank higher on depression, anxiety, impulsive and insomnia levels than those who don't.

Moreover, another level of research shows that frequently using social media is directly related to high rates of depression. The more Facebook you use, the more your satisfaction levels

---

[4] https://wb.md/3y80Hwf

in life decline.[5]

An important thing to note here is that spending more time on the internet also pulls you into the comparison trap. You compare yourself and your life with others, complain about what you don't have and lack gratitude for your life. Moreover, it also kills your time and love with your family. When you remain hooked to the phone, laptop, X-box, or any other gadget for long, you are distancing yourself from all those who truly love you.[6]

All these problems only devour your willpower, reducing your drive to discipline yourself. Want to feel better? Go on a digital detox from time to time.

- Set a time limit to use your phone or laptop when you are not using it for work. If you watch movies on it for entertainment, set an hour in the day for it, and shut down your computer when the hour is over.
- Create a time window to check your email, messages, and calls only. If you have decided to check your phone for messages from 5 pm to 5:15 pm, put your phone down at sharp 5:15 pm.
- Set reminders and alarms to ensure you stick to the time windows.
- Designate an area of your room as tech-free/gadget-free, and every time you step in it, ditch your phone, laptop, tablet, and other gadgets.
- Slowly adopt the habit of putting away your gadgets at least an hour before your bedtime, so you unwind and find it easier to doze off.

---

[5] https://www.newportacademy.com/resources/restoring-families/digital-detox/
[6] https://www.newportacademy.com/resources/restoring-families/digital-detox/

- After a few weeks of trying these practices, go on a digital detox for a full day, a day dedicated to not using any device or gadget at all.
- After some time, go on a two to three-day digital detox, and then execute it once a month regularly.
- Ensure that you pay close attention to your stress levels and the ability to practice self-control before and after taking all these measures. That way, you will understand how beneficial digital detoxes are for you.

You have great power and potential. The various techniques and practices discussed in this book only seek to help you regain your strength and energy, so you don't waste it on things that don't matter, and invest your time and energy it in substantial goals that build towards progress and help you reach your goals.

CONCLUSION

I am extremely thankful to you for investing your valuable time in read this book. But more importantly, you must thank yourself for taking a big step in learning this system for fighting back against your self-saboteur. You made it this far, and now, you have the tools, courage and guidance to take it the rest of the way. It fills me with a level of deep satisfaction to have created something empowering for you because you truly deserve this.

The ball has always been in your court. You have always had the power in you to set things right. The difference is that now, you realize that power. Now that you do, it is time to do things right. It is time to take hold of this inner power and use it to cultivate your most disciplined self.

You have got this! And this book is your blueprint to make sure you keep embarking on powerful journeys and make the best use of your time, energy, and life.

When you have hard days (and you will) remember what you learned here. Refer back to the Bite the Bullet framework, take a deep breath, meditate on where you are at and, visualize a point in the future you want to go. Point your sails in that direction and keep moving.

The journey is unfolding. You're the captain of your own ship, taking control of destiny, and there is no stopping you now.

I'll see you on that other side,
Scott Allan

"The secret of success is learning how to use pain and pleasure instead of having pain and pleasure use you. If you don't, life controls you."